Bronze Boar Figurines in Iron Age and Roman Britain

Jennifer Foster

British Archaeological Reports 39
1977

British Archaeological Reports

122, Banbury Road, Oxford OX2 7BP, England

B.A.R. 39, 1977: "Bronze Boar Figurines in Iron Age and Roman Britain"

ISBN 9780904531749 paperback

ISBN 9781407320496 e-book

DOI https://doi.org/10.30861/9780904531749

A catalogue record for this book is available from the British Library

This book is available at www.barpublishing.com

CONTENTS

LIST OF FIGURES

LIST OF PLATES

INTRODUCTION

The boar has been venerated, eulogised, hunted and eaten in Europe for millennia, until its virtual extinction in recent historical time. This admiration revealed itself in British myths long after the pagan Celtic period, and the boar's head was still an important dish in Medieval England. The attention paid to the boar, therefore, was not confined to the barbarian Celtic peoples of Northern Europe (there are many bronze amulets of boars from Classical Greece for example), or to the period in which the Celts as a people were most widespread, in the centuries leading up to Roman domination. The boar figurines from Britain show that the animal is a recurring feature in the Roman as well as the Pre-Roman period. Celtic boar representations are not over-numerous, and the figure of the boar is by no means restricted to Celtic contexts.

There can, however, be no doubt that the boar was an important animal in late prehistoric Europe. There is for example, archaeological evidence of deposits of pig haunches in graves, presumably intended as offerings of food to carry the deceased to the afterlife. From the little of what we know of Iron Age religion, chiefly from the classical references, it seems that belief in an afterlife formed a fairly central part of the traditions. Many of the Yorkshire Arras graves, for example (Greenwell, 1906) contain pig bones. At Arras itself, although most graves contained only a humerus, two foreparts and two heads were discovered, and in one barrow at Danes Graves, an entire skeleton was found. The pig remains were often closely associated with the body, lying close to the face or covering the shoulders. Another example of the importance of pig bones in grave offerings comes from a Belgic cremation grave at Snailwell, Cambridgeshire, (Lethbridge, 1953), where the complete skeleton of a pig accompanied the burial. On the continent, many of the La Tène burials in the Champàgne area of France contain pig bones (Stead, 1965: 77). A cemetery at Soporon-Becsidom, Hungary, produced many interments with joints of pork, and a whole boar was buried separately in one stone-lined grave (Szabo, 1971:68).

It has been suggested (Stead 1965:77) that the inclusion of pig may have formed part of the religious ceremony. Perhaps the offering took the form of food provision for the future life; thus the comment by Greenwell in his discussion of the Yorkshire graves, "The pig therefore appears to have been the favourite animal in the dietary of these people, if provision made for the dead may be taken as an index of the taste of the living". (1906:265). This does not of course imply that pork was a frequently eaten meat; on the contrary, this deference for pig contrasts with what must have been its proportionate importance in the diet. In Britain, pig forms a minor, though consistent, percentage of the fauna on most pre-Roman Iron Age sites, taking third place to cattle and sheep, and representing, on average,

TABLE 1

PIG BONES FROM ARCHAEOLOGICAL SITES

SITE	REFERENCE	PIG %	PIG Nos.	COW %	COW Nos.	SHEEP %	SHEEP Nos.
Angle Ditch, Dorset	Pitt-Rivers, A., 1887:58	---	---	67	---	13	---
Bagendon, Glos	Clifford, E., 1961:268	Frags		Numerous		Present	
Bathampton Down, Somerset	Wainwright, G., 1967:57	6	7	---	69	---	39
Beckford, Worc.	Oswald, A., 1972:18	6	27	31	134	27	115
		16	*6	23	*7	39	*12
Blaise Castle, Bristol	Rahtz, P., and Brown, J., 1959:170	19	11	12	7	67	39
Breedon-on-the-Hill, Leics.	Wacher, J. S., 1964	8	5	47	28	33	20
Catcote, Northumberland	Hodgson, G., 1961:136	9.1	*3	54.6	*8	39.6	*6
Coygan Camp, Caernarvon	Wainwright, G., 1967	15	97	64	381	16	101
Clickhimin, Shetland	Hamilton, J., 1968:166	1	1	66	60	31	28
Croft Ambrey, Hereford	Stanford, S., 1974:216	33.5	(mean)	29	(mean)	37.5	(mean)
Eldon's Seat, Dorset	Cunliffe, B., 1968:226 a.	3.5	35	50.6	508	40.7	408
	b.	6.4	31	28.3	140	61.7	305
	c.	4.4	66	43.3	648	47.7	713
Glastonbury, Somerset	Stanford, S., 1974:221	1.6	---	5.7	---	92.7	---
Grimthorpe, Yorkshire	Stead, I., 1968:183	7.8	57	54.9	403	25	184
Hawk's Hill, Surrey	Hastings, F., 166:40	20-22	---	17-21	---	56-7	---
Hod Hill, Dorset	Richmond, I., 1968:123	16	26	19	31	65	107
Jarlshof, Shetland	Hamilton, J., 1956:212	Few		Numerous		Numerous	
Maiden Castle, Dorset	Wheeler, R. E. M., 1943:369	Few		Numerous		Numerous	
Martin Down, Dorset	Pitt-Rivers, A., 1887:185	9	---	66	---	13	---
Old Sleaford, Lincolnshire	Higgs, E., and White, J., 1963:282	28	*14	14	*7	54	*27
Portsdown Hill, Hampshire	Bradley, R., 1968:53	5	---	65	---	25	---
Rainsborough Camp, Northamptonshire	Avery, M., et. al., 1967:304 a.	13	---	39	---	48	---
	b.	12	---	38	---	50	---
	c.	21	---	34	---	44	---
Shenbarrow, Gloucestershire	Fell, C., 1961:37	21	15	39	28	35	25
South Lodge Camp, Dorset	Pitt-Rivers, A., 1887:1	1	---	48	---	16	---
Sutton Walls, Hereford	Kenyon, K., 1953:1	15.2	360	52.7	929	32.1	508
Stanwick, Yorkshire	Stanford, S., 1974:221	20.3	---	50.6	---	29.1	---
Tollard Royal, Wiltshire	Wainwright, G., 1968:123	6	---	31	---	6	---

Percentages given first, then absolute numbers of bones. Where these are not available, minimum numbers of species given (marked thus: *)

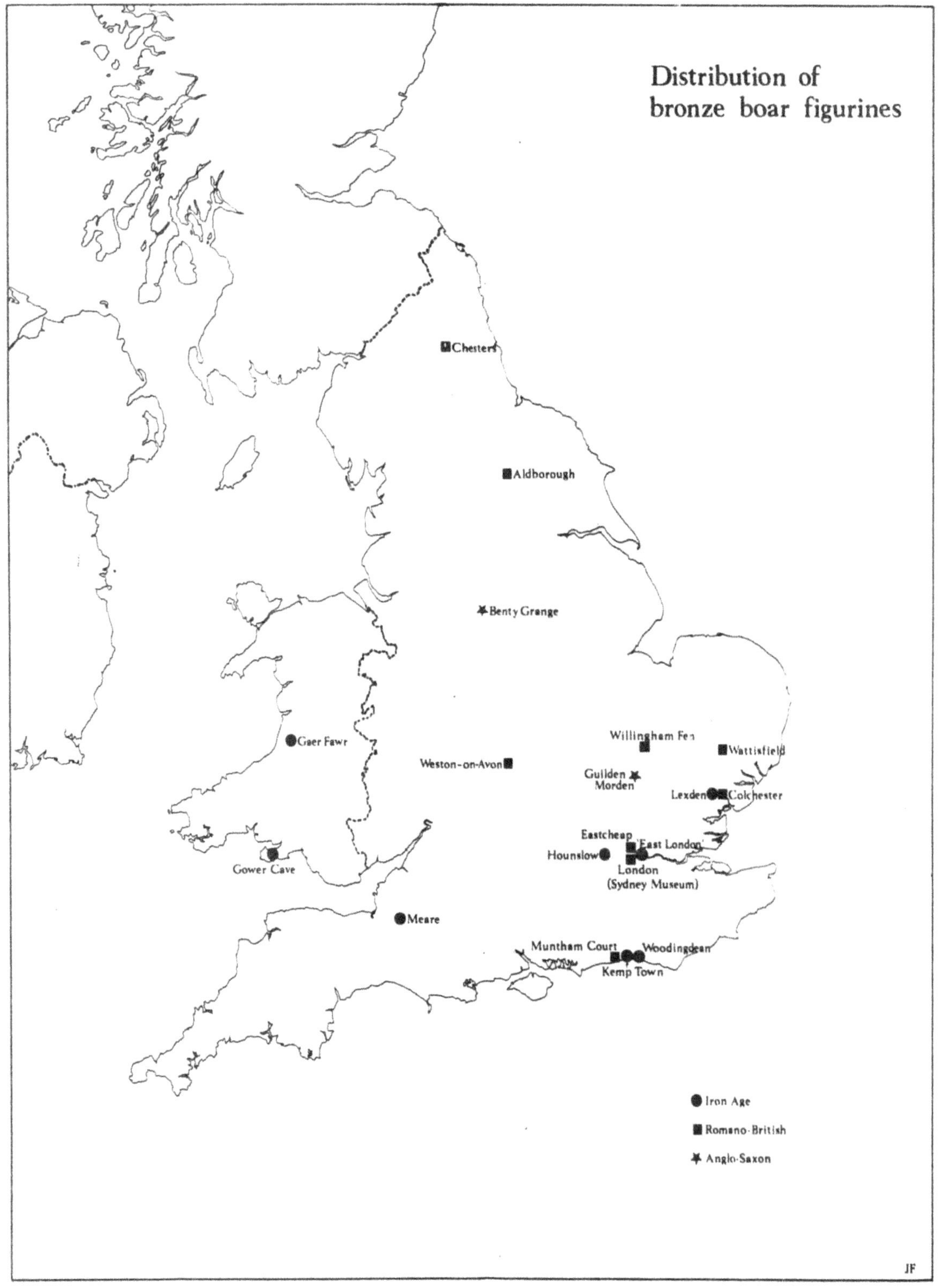

Fig. 1 Distribution of bronze boar figurines in Britain.

15% of the total bone fragments (Table 1). Pigs were possibly more difficult to raise as a meat animal than were sheep and cattle; the choice of pig as a grave offering may imply therefore that pork was regarded as something of a delicacy.

Nevertheless, pigs held a position of importance in the ideology of the Celts which should not be under estimated. Certain comments of the classical writers imply that the boar was used as a totemic object. Tacitus for example mentions in Germania that the Celtic Aestii wore amulets of the wild boar, said to be sacred to the mother goddess, to protect them from harm in battle. (Germania, Book 45). Diodorus Siculus wrote of the Celts, "Their armour includes man sized shields, decorated in individual fashion. Some of these have projecting bronze animals of fine workmanship which serve for defence as well as decoration. On their heads they wear bronze helmets which possess large projecting figures, lending the appearance of enormous stature to the wearer; in some cases horns form one piece with the helmet, while in other cases, it is relief figures of the foreparts of birds or quadrupeds." (quoted: Tierney, 1960:251). It is generally presumed that these figurines were intended to protect the wearer from harm by carrying an emblem of the god. Many writers referring to the European bronze boar figurines have assumed their Celtic origin and pointed to them as examples of helmet crests. (Gray and Bulleid made this suggestion in 1955: Vol. II, 223). There are no archaeological examples of helmets with boars actually attached except one of Anglo-Saxon date from Benty Grange, Derbyshire (see below, page 23).

The great silver cauldron from Gundestrup, probably depicting Celtic ideology, though its place of manufacture is uncertain, provides further evidence of boar-crested helmets. On one of the inner plates (E) a scene shows four riding figures each with helmets topped with a feather crest, horns, a boar and a bird respectively. Below are foot soldiers, one of whom wears a helmet also surmounted with a boar. (Klindt-Jensen, 1961; Powell, 1971). Werner (1949;254) mentions a later bronze plate from Torslund, Öland, Sweden, showing warriors in relief with boars on their helmets; this is of the Migration period. The boar was evidently used in another war context, as the mouthpiece for the Celtic war trumpet, or carnyx: the same plate of the Gundestrup Cauldron (E) shows three men blowing trumpets with boar terminals. These were probably similar to the trumpets referred to by Diodorus Siculus (translated: Tierney 1960:251), "Their trumpets again are of a peculiar barbaric kind; they blow into them and produce a harsh sound which suits the tumult of war." A sheet metal boar's head found at Deskford, Banffshire in 1816, was shown conclusively by Piggott (1959) to have been a carnyx mouthpiece, like those on the coins of the Catuvellauni (Mack, 1964: No. 223). Coins of the British pre-Roman Iron Age frequently carry reliefs of boars, particularly those of Tasciovanus, Cunobelin, Dubnovellaunus and the Iceni (Piggott, 1959).

That the boar was of consequence to the Celts therefore is clear. What is interesting is that the situation changed with the Roman period. The boar became one among many of the species portrayed by the Roman artists, including exotic non-European animals. Its importance in the Iron Age period is exposed by the exclusiveness of the Celtic choice; only boar, ox, ram and certain birds were chosen to be portrayed in significant numbers.

Meare, Somerset

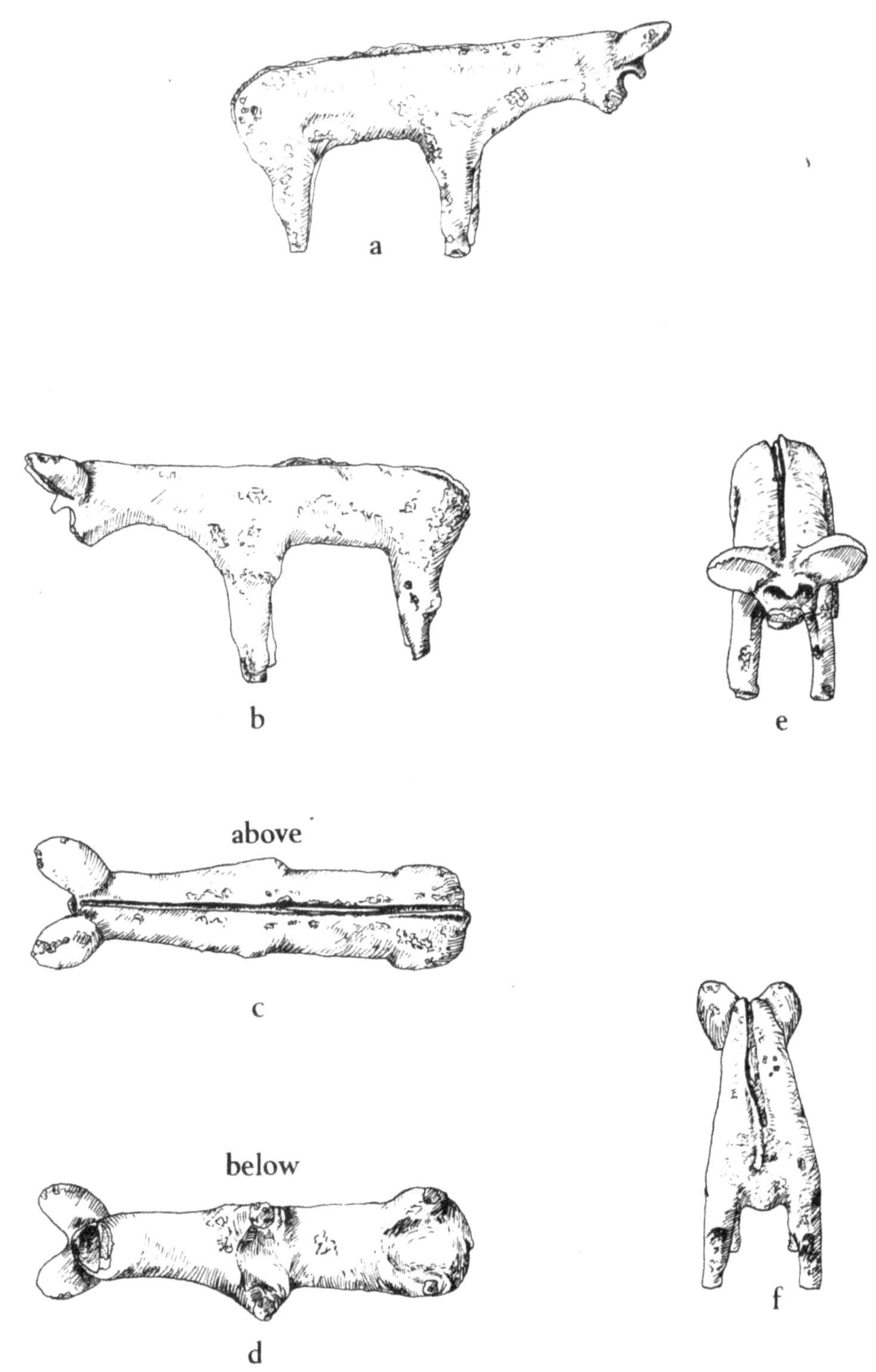

Fig. 2 Boar figurine from Meare, Somerset. c: showing groove along the back.

BOARS OF IRON AGE DATE

We have seen that the boar is found in a wide range of contexts in Europe in the pre-Roman Iron Age and later (Cf. Werner, 1949). It has been the custom to compare the British bronze boar figurines with others from the continent, the well known examples of which are Celtic in style and presumably pre-Roman Iron Age in date. The continental boars in a "Celtic" style are well illustrated by the boar from Bata, Hungary, with an exaggerated and decorative spinal crest (Cf. Jacobsthal, 1944: No. 371). This is frequently compared to the boar from Hounslow (B, Fig. 5), typical Celtic features being the openwork crest (no longer intact on the Hounslow example), and the highly stylised manner of the design. The ability to abstract certain features, e.g. the legs, and to elaborate others, particularly the crest and enormous ears, is characteristic of the Celtic art style. Very few of the boars may be dated on stylistic grounds by drawing parallels with objects on the continent, a situation not aided by the fact that few, here or abroad, have proper associations in stratified contexts.

Twenty-two bronze boar figurines from Britain are known to the writer. They are both Iron Age and Roman in date, and of these only three are stratified, and two are now lost. It will be appreciated that this raises a number of problems in accurately dating the objects.

Of the pre-Roman Iron Age boars with some sort of association, that from Meare Lake Village, Somerset is probably the earliest figurine found in Britain (Fig. 2). The boar is described in the text (Gray and Bulleid, 1953:223) as found on the second floor of Mound XV. On the plan, however, (Plate XXXI) it is shown on Mound XIII, and No. 53 (bronze boar) is included in the list of objects said to have come from Mound XIII not XV. This mistake is no doubt due to overlapping of the mounds. The amount of Roman material from the site was negligible, and on stylistic grounds alone it seems reasonable to ascribe the figurine to the pre-Roman Iron Age; the enormous ears and stocky unshaped legs show no signs of Roman influence.

The site was originally dated to c. 150 B.C. until the Roman conquest, being included with Glastonbury in the Third Southwestern B of Hawkes' scheme (1959), on the basis of the pottery and various imported metal objects. Most of the fibulae are La Tène III type, including a developed La Tène III Nauheim fibula, with only one La Tène II and one La Tène I fibulae (Gray and Bulleid, 1953: Vol. 2, 205-208). A coin found in the recent excavations (Avery, 1968) was identified by D. F. Allen as Breton, probably a billon of the Corosolites; similar coins occur in the La Catillon hoard, c. 50 B.C. (Allen, 1958). This tends to confirm the overall impression that occupation at Meare began during the third century B.C., and expanded as Avery suggests, in the second century, the majority of the finds falling between 150 B.C. and c. 1 B.C. The boar is likely to have reached the site therefore during the later part of the pre-Roman Iron Age.

The only other boar found in an undoubtedly pre-Roman context (Figs. 3 and 4) is that from the Lexden Tumulus, Colchester, Essex (Laver, 1927 and Foster, in preparation). The figurine has been dated to the Belgic

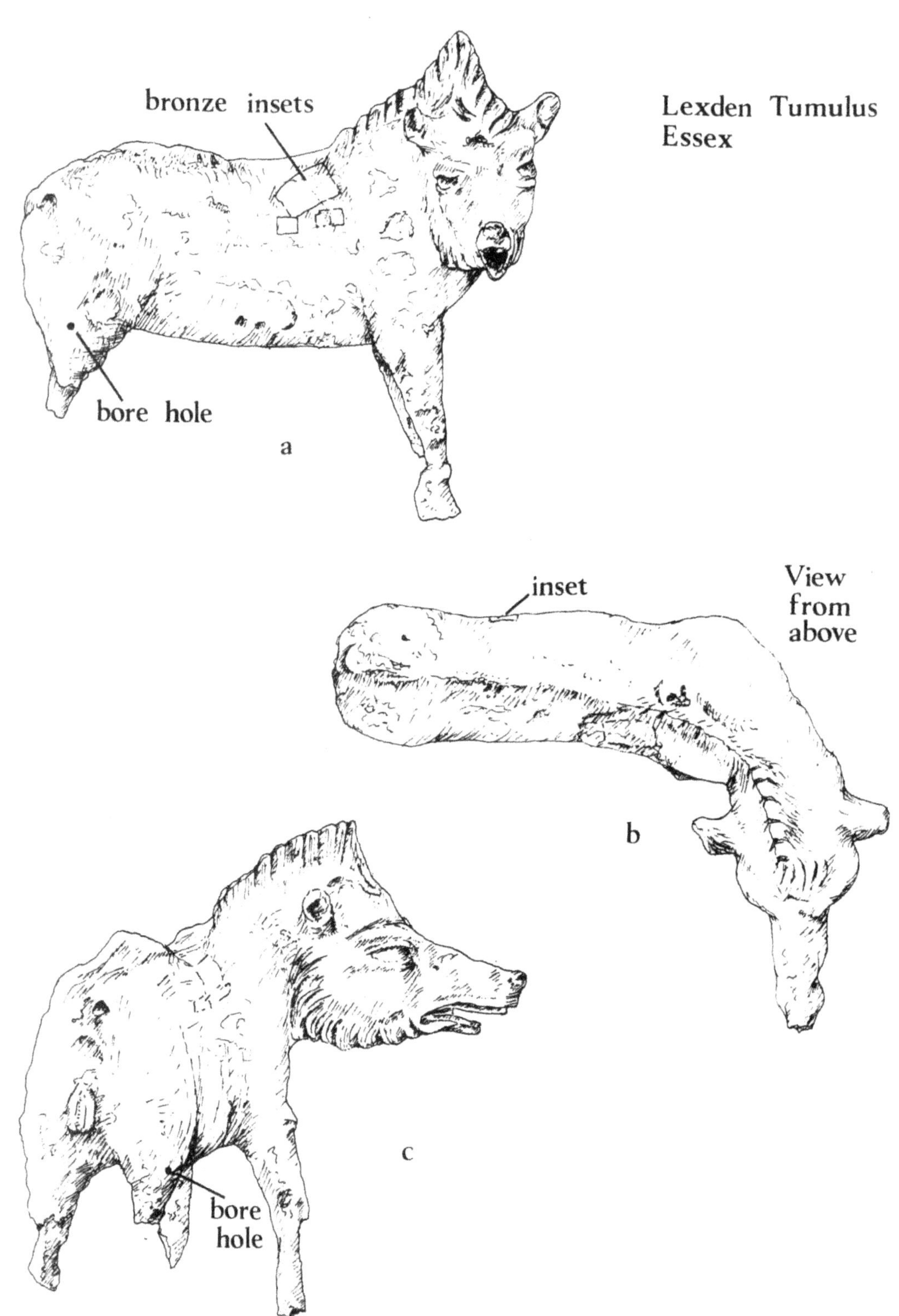

Fig. 3 Three views of boar figurine from Lexden Tumulus, Essex. Scale 1:1.

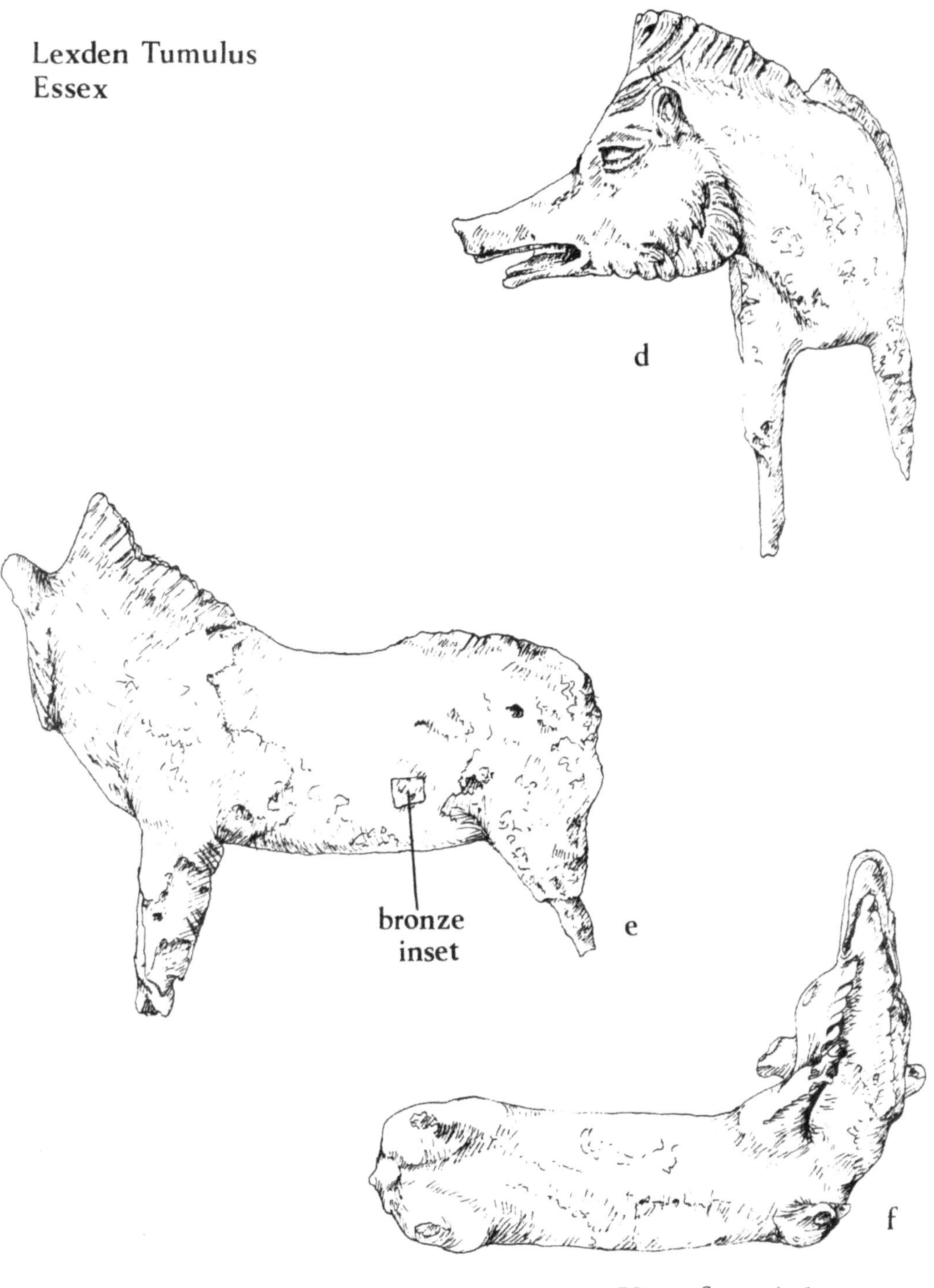

Fig. 4 Three views of boar figurine from Lexden Tumulus, Essex. Scale 1:1.

period (Megaw, 1963, 32), and Toynbee regards it as Gaulish, as it resembles closely the sow from Cahors, and the boar from Luxembourg (Continental Catalogue, Nos. 4 and 10; Toynbee, 1964:39).

It is conceivable that the boar was made and imported from the Roman world, particularly as many of the other objects from the tumulus are probably imports. The old theory that Lexden was the grave of Cunobelin, and dated therefore to c. 40 A.D., has been criticised by Peacock (1971) as a result of his study of the amphorae from the Tumulus. He felt that the burial would be more reasonably dated to the last 15 years B.C., which would coincide well with the date of a silver medallion of Augustus, also found in the grave, minted in 17 B.C. and in excellent condition. Peacock concluded that if the tumulus was raised in 40 A.D., the Dressel 1 amphorae, in particular, would be archaic additions to the grave. Recent finds of amphorae in the Drammont D shipwreck in the Mediterranean, however, (Liou, 1973:595-8) show that Dressel 5 and Rhodian amphorae, paralleled in the Lexden grave, were still being carried in 40-50 A.D. The date for the cargo is based on Arretine pottery and pottery lamps. Although Dressel 1 amphorae were not exported from Italy after c. 15 B.C., it is conceivable that they reached Britain later. It is therefore difficult to give a more precise date for the grave than that proposed in the original publication, c. 15 B.C. - 40 A.D.

Further evidence which confirms a general date in the later pre-Roman Iron Age is provided by a quantitative analysis of the various metal components in the boar, the pedestal and one of the pins from Lexden (Werner and Craddock, 1971). Most Roman statuary of the first century A.D. contained at least 6% lead and about 10% tin. The analyses proved the pedestal to be of classical origin, as expected, and the bronze of the stud unquestionably Celtic manufacture (although for an analysis of the red enamel see Hughes, 1972). The composition of the boar is similar to that of the stud; apparently it would be unusual, but not unique, for a Roman bronze. Because of its rather representational style compared with the other Iron Age examples, the possibility of Roman manufacture cannot be ruled out, however. It is interesting to note the change in style that took place between the manufacture of the typically 'Celtic' boars, and that from Lexden. I would accept Kendrick's contrast between the abstraction of the Hounslow boar and the naturalism of the Lexden one (1938:14). This boar is one of the finest examples of Roman style metalwork discovered in Britain.

The three most famous British boars, of undoubted Iron Age date, were recovered by labourers from a field near Hounslow in 1864. They were presented to the British Museum in the same year. The animals have been praised many times for the care of their design, typical of the Celtic style; Megaw for example makes the following comment, "The Hounslow animals ... are made to a formula, but a formula which is based on a careful distillation of the essential elements of nature". (1970, 139). These boars are sometimes held to be similar to continental boar figurines but the first, Hounslow A (Fig. 5) is unique, and has no close parallels; except that is, for the generally abstracted nature of its design, the emphasised crest and eye. The figurine appears to have had some kind of stand, which

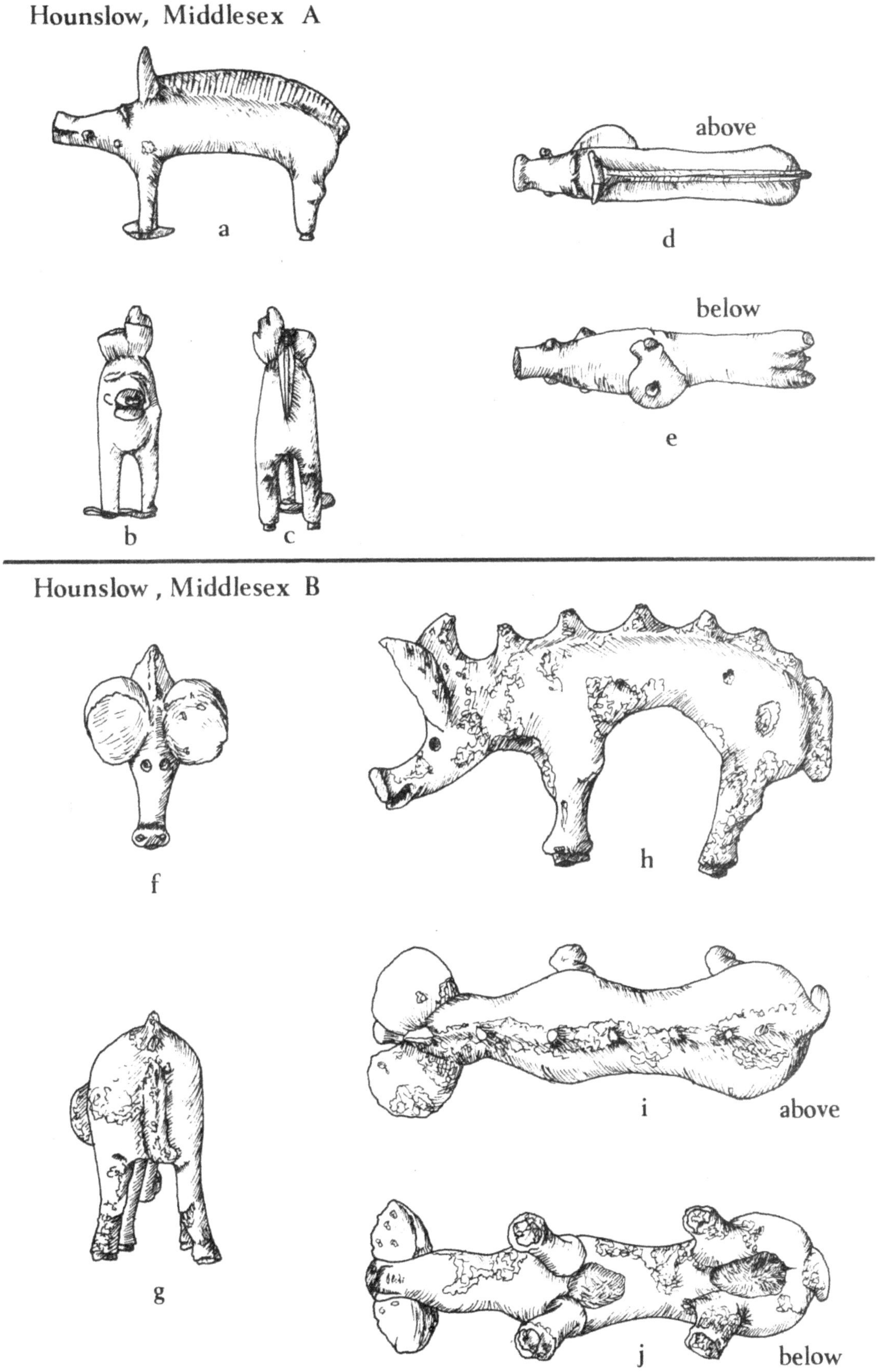

Hounslow, Middlesex A

a

above

d

below

e

b

c

Hounslow , Middlesex B

f

h

g

i

above

j

below

Fig. 5 Boar figurines A and B from Hounslow, Middlesex. Scale 1:1.

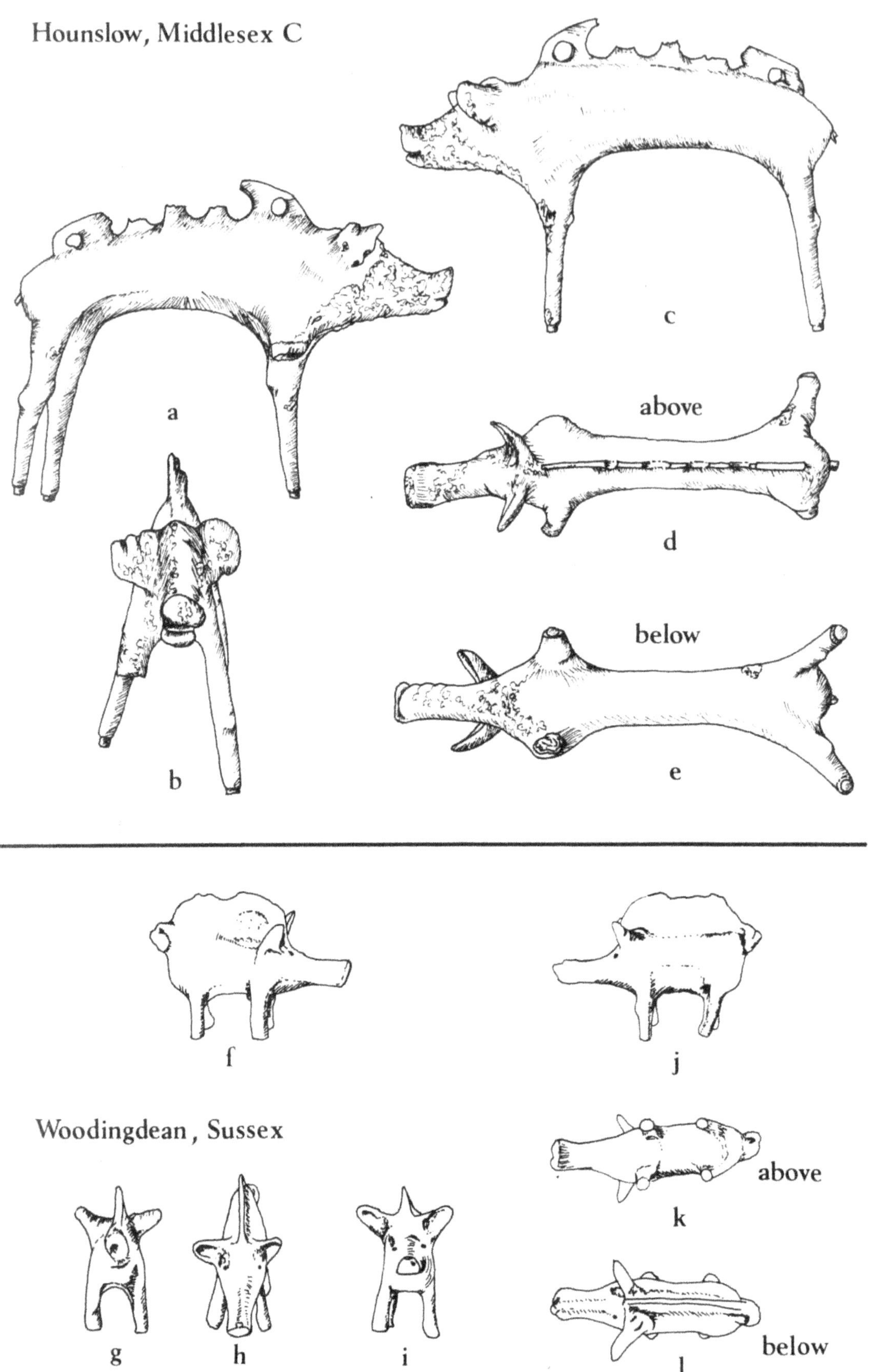

Fig. 6 Boar figurines C from Hounslow, Middlesex, and boar figurine from Woodingdean, Sussex. Scale 1:1.

indicates that the figure was free-standing; most of this has now perished. Hounslow B (Fig. 5) has been discussed by many different authors and is comparable to a number of boars on the continent, particularly those from Bata and Luncani. It has attracted a great deal of admiration, being, according to Toynbee, "as abstract as any representational works of art can be... (expressing) in simple sophisticated terms, the rant build and relentless vigour of these creatures". (1964:24). The great crest which is such a prominent feature of Celtic boar figurines, though not as elaborate as that from Luncani, and now broken, helps to justify the remarks that have been made about this figure. In terms of aesthetic appeal, it is clumsy compared to Hounslow C (below), with a carelessly modelled tail and snout; it does not convey the character of the boar, which is so delightfully displayed in the superb caricature from Woodingdean. There can be no doubt, however, that the Celtic craftsman has surpassed himself in this figure in reducing the boar to its barest essentials - crest, ears and snout.

Hounslow C (Fig. 6) is a delicate figurine, more carefully cast than many of the boars from Europe, whose charm lies rather in weight and stocky features. The crest, originally openwork with punched holes, is now unfortunately broken but enough remains for its reconstruction. Unlike many of the figurines, this still retains the original surface on its flanks and crest, where marks of filing can be seen. This figurine is generally ignored in discussions of the Hounslow boars, and yet is as sensitive as any Celtic work of art.

Fox felt that the Hounslow boars were definitely designed as helmet crests, indeed boars B and C have slight "pegs" on all four feet. More probably the intention was for them to be fixed onto stands like Hounslow A. It is possible that Hounslow C was designed for suspension. A similar boar from Joeuvres oppidum in the Loire, France, for example, is provided with two holes through the crest, and although this may be purely decoration, Déchelette felt that it was an amulet to be hung around the neck (Déchelette, 1927, IV, 813). A more convincing example of this is that from the Altenburg - Rheinau oppidum, a crudely cast animal with a ring above the tail (Fischer, 1974, 159).

Of the other supposedly Iron Age boars, only one has any association which might help with dating. That from Woodingdean, near Brighton, Sussex, (Fig. 6) is said to have been found with a swan's neck pin (Curwen, 1954, Fig. 72). This is most similar to the developed local British pin, with a plain head bent at right angles to the stem. The closest parallel is the one from Woodeaton, Oxfordshire (Dunning, 1935). These pins are dated to before the third century B.C., and stylistically there is no difficulty in placing the boar in that period. Although it is not typical of the developed La Tène figurines, I would agree with Leeds that it is the best of the British Iron Age boars.

Two other Sussex boars have been given an Iron Age, or at least a pre-Roman date. One was recorded by Mr. Toms (Toms, 1907 and 1918) as being found by a market gardener whilst digging in his garden behind St. Mary's Hall, Kemp Town, Brighton, in the decade before 1918. The gardener was an avid collector of antiquities, including Roman pottery,

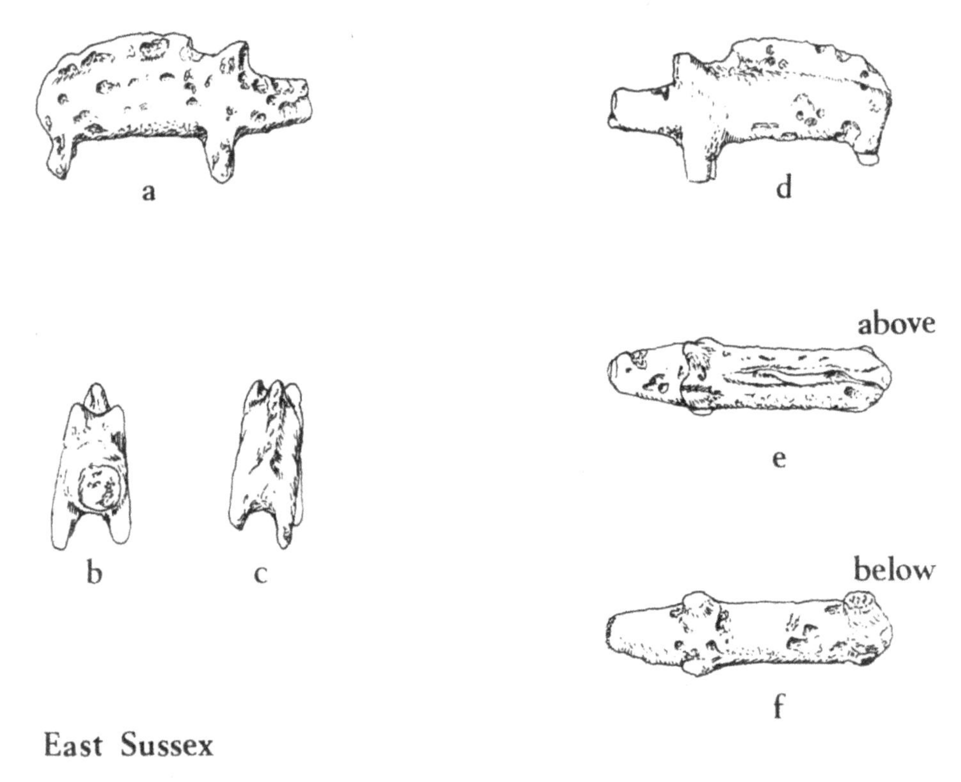

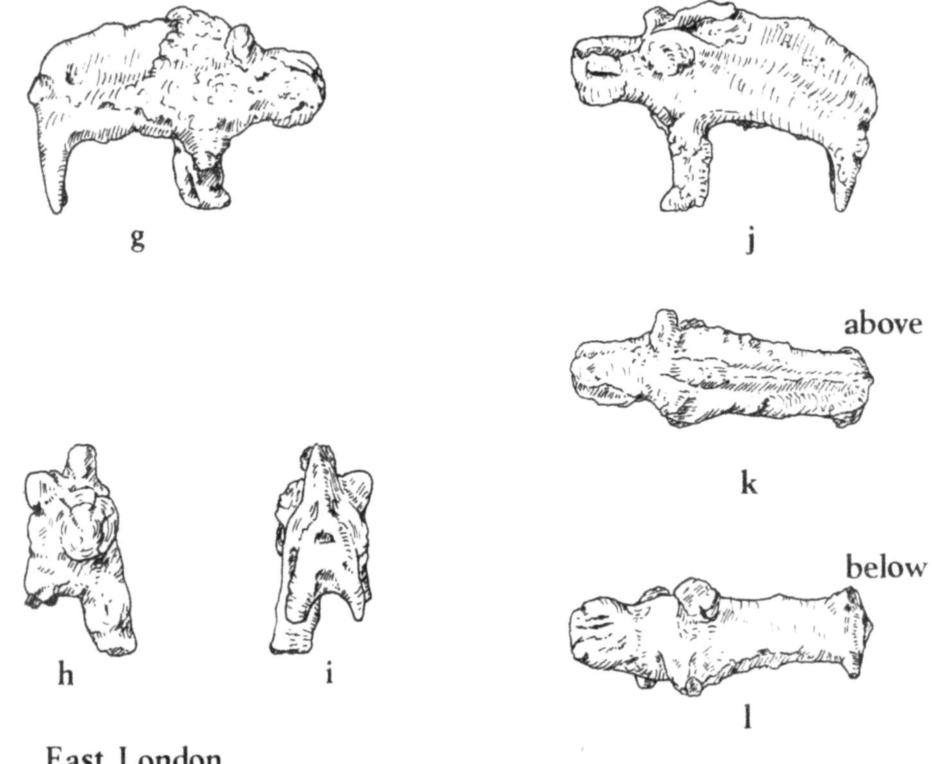

Fig. 7 Boar figurines from East Sussex and East London. Scale 1:1.

coins and brooches, but the boar was apparently lost without trace soon after discovery. Mr. Toms expressed a hope that "it would come to light when the garden was dug over again". (1918, 4). Toms compared it favourably with the Woodingdean boar; it was said to be of a similar size, but this must remain unsubstantiated. Other finds from the site include Romano-British pottery and a fibula. The site is probably a small rural farm of the type that cover the South Downs and where, invariably, Iron Age occupation continues with little change into the Roman period (Cunliffe, 1973:96).

Even more elusive is the boar from "East Sussex", now in Barbican House Museum, Lewes (Fig. 7) which has no associations or known provenance. The date of its arrival at the Museum and the identity of the donor are also unknown, although it must have been received after 1866 when the antiquities in the castle were catalogued (Lower and Chapman, 1866), and it was known to Toms in 1907 (489-90). It has been ascribed to the Iron Age, however, and there seems no reason to doubt this on the basis of style. The crudeness of the casting and the corrosion due to active bronze disease makes further comment impossible.

Another figurine of unknown provenance, closely similar to the Lewes boar, is in the Roach Smith collection in the British Museum. It is said to have been found in East London in 1865, and was in the British Museum in 1930 (Vulliamy, 1930:134). A rather shapeless animal, partially hidden by extensive corrosion, it would be only tentatively recognised as a boar were it not for its resemblance to the Lewes boar. (Fig. 7).

An indeterminate animal, obviously intended to represent a boar, has been in the Ashmolean Museum, Oxford, since 1931, with no more information attached to it than that it came from Gower Cave, Rhossilly, Glamorganshire (Fig. 8). Professor Grimes informs me (private communication) that the cave is one of a series on the Gower Peninsula, which were dug into by a number of people in the early part of this century, producing finds of all periods from the Palaeolithic onwards. The boar has therefore no exact provenance and no associations. It appears to be unpublished, although it was mentioned by Gray and Bulleid (1953:224).

The other boar figurine from Wales is also unstratified and without associations. In 1911 it was privately owned by Major Myton from Barth, Guilsfield, and it was said to have been dug up in the garden of 26 Severn Street, Welshpool. This in fact is the same figurine as that published by the Rev. Barnwell in 1871 (pp. 163-7), and found "some years ago within an ancient work in Montgomeryshire, called Gaer-Fawr," which was owned by Major Myton at that time. The boar was considered by Barnwell to have "none of the outlines of animal form so common in Celtic work, but instead thereof a wonderful amount of fidelity and spirit found in good production of Roman art". He had no doubt as to its origins: it was a representation of the Twentieth Legion's badge (see below, p. 19). In fact Gaer Fawr is a multivallate hillfort (Map of Southern Britain in the Iron Age, Ref. SJ 224130). The style of this boar is too crude to be typically Roman, and with the long incision along its belly (Fig. 8 and Plate IVc) seems better fitted as a Celtic helmet emblem, than the legionary badge of a Roman soldier.

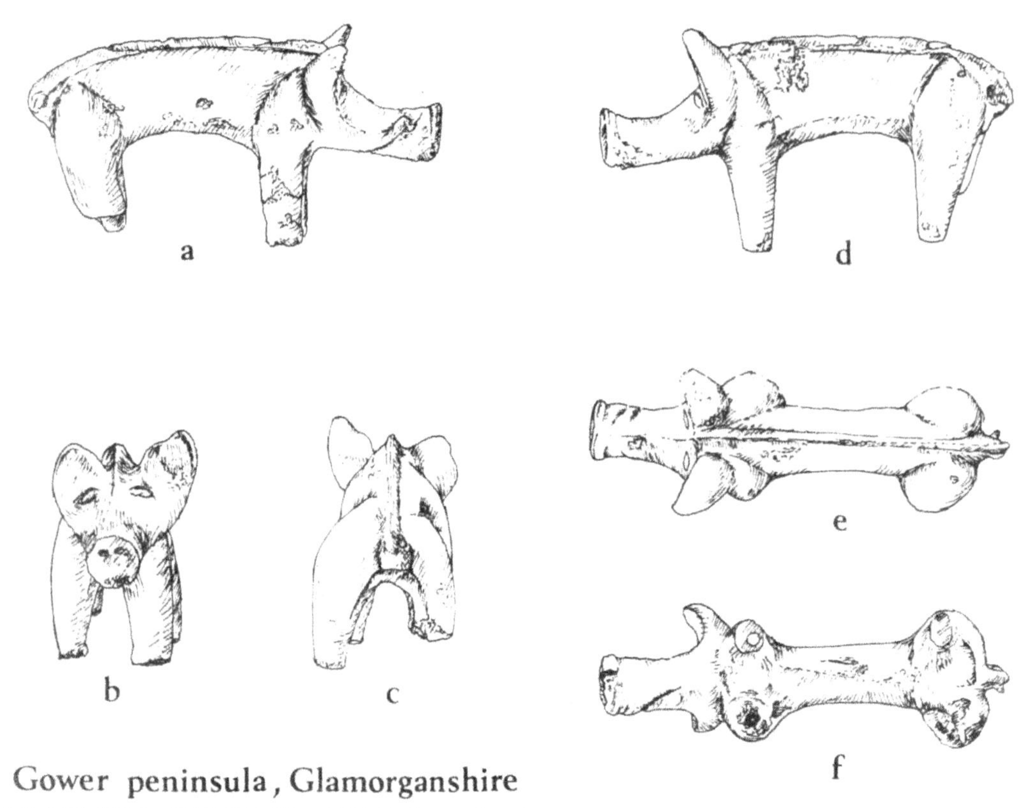

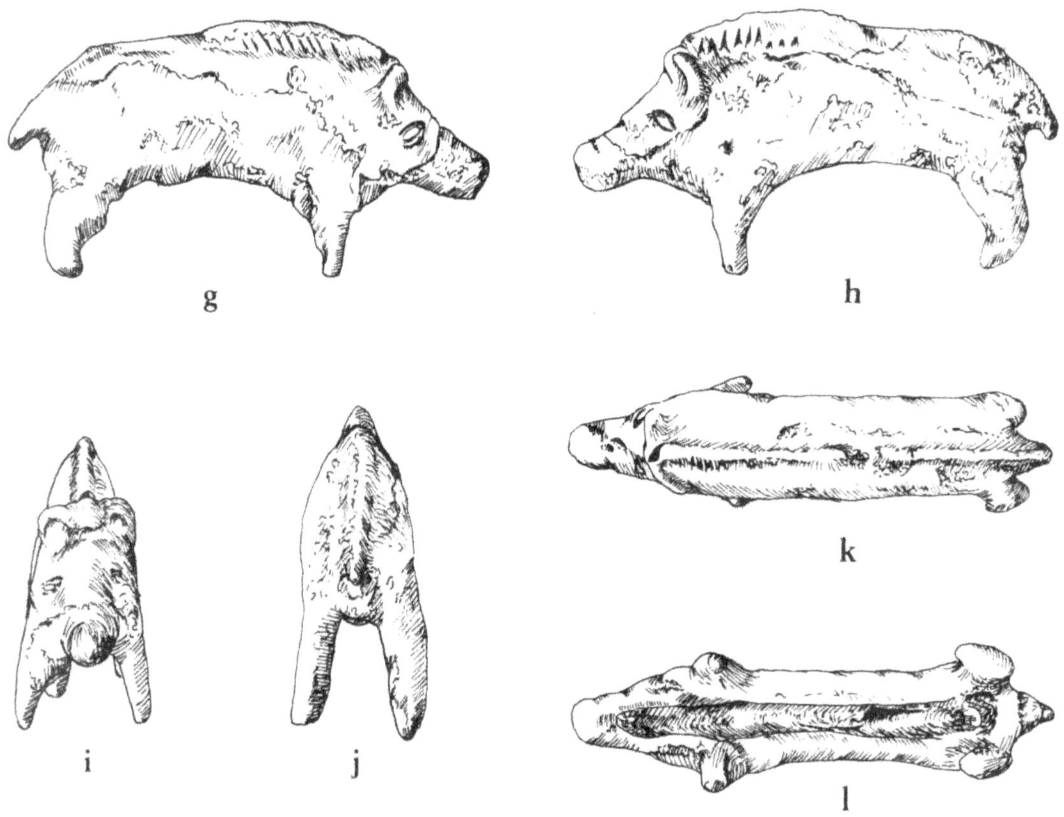

Fig. 8 Boar figurines from Gower peninsula, Glamorganshire and Gaer Fawr, Montgomeryshire. Scale 1:1.

BOARS OF ROMAN DATE

The only well stratified Roman boar was found during the excavation of a Romano-Celtic Temple at Muntham Court, Findon, Sussex, in 1954. (Fig. 9). The excavators discovered a large complex of Early Iron Age post holes, in parallel rows similar to other Iron Age settlements in the area, with other evidence for Iron Age occupation. A part of the site was levelled in the Romano-British period and a circular shrine constructed, in front of which accumulated a rubbish dump of Romano-British date, covering earlier features. Various bronze objects were recovered from this dump, including four first century A.D. brooches, one very worn second century A.D. coin, a bronze fish decorated in blue and green enamel, and the boar. The pottery dates from the first to the early fourth centuries A.D. (Burstow and Holleyman, 1957). Most of the finds are obviously domestic refuse, which seems to suggest that the boar, too, was rubbish from a domestic building. As the excavation was fairly small in area, it may be that buildings of the Romano-British period, from which the boar could have derived, lay outside the area excavated. Equally probable is that the boar had some practical purpose, rather than being a "votive offering". It can be compared with the two plaques in the form of lions from Capel St. Mary, Suffolk, (Moore, 1947, 166), also of Roman date (second century A.D.). Like the Muntham boar they have a flat front and a hollow back, and were attached to some object by two iron bars or rivets, portions of which still remain. (One is illustrated, Plate VIII). They were presumably furniture decorations, a suggestion made plausible by the fact that they were found in the remains of a town house, together with window glass, plaster and other objects. The Muntham plaque has no obvious means of attachment, but the degree of wear on the surface is commensurate with such use. Another plaque in the form of a boar, from Wattisfield, Suffolk, can be compared to the Muntham boar. This was dug up in a field during land drainage operations in 1943 (Moore, 1947: 168) and is therefore without associations; it is however Roman in style. The surface of the object is heavily worn (Fig. 9), as if it were attached to some articles of clothing; a plausible use in view of its size.

If its exact function cannot be determined, the Muntham boar can at least be placed firmly within the Roman period. From the point of view of style, however, the boar is not altogether characteristic of Roman art, the design being reminiscent of Celtic imagery. A similar observation can be extended to the Capel St. Mary lions (Toynbee, 1964:122). Toynbee reflects this when she says of the Muntham Court boar; "it effectively harmonizes naturalism in its general aspect with specifically Celtic features - the curiously drawn-up hind legs, the abnormally large snout, and the conspicuously decorated dorsal bristles". (1964:126, and plate XXXIII).

It is possible that the boar was connected with the shrine and had some sort of cult significance. One might even conjecture that it repres-

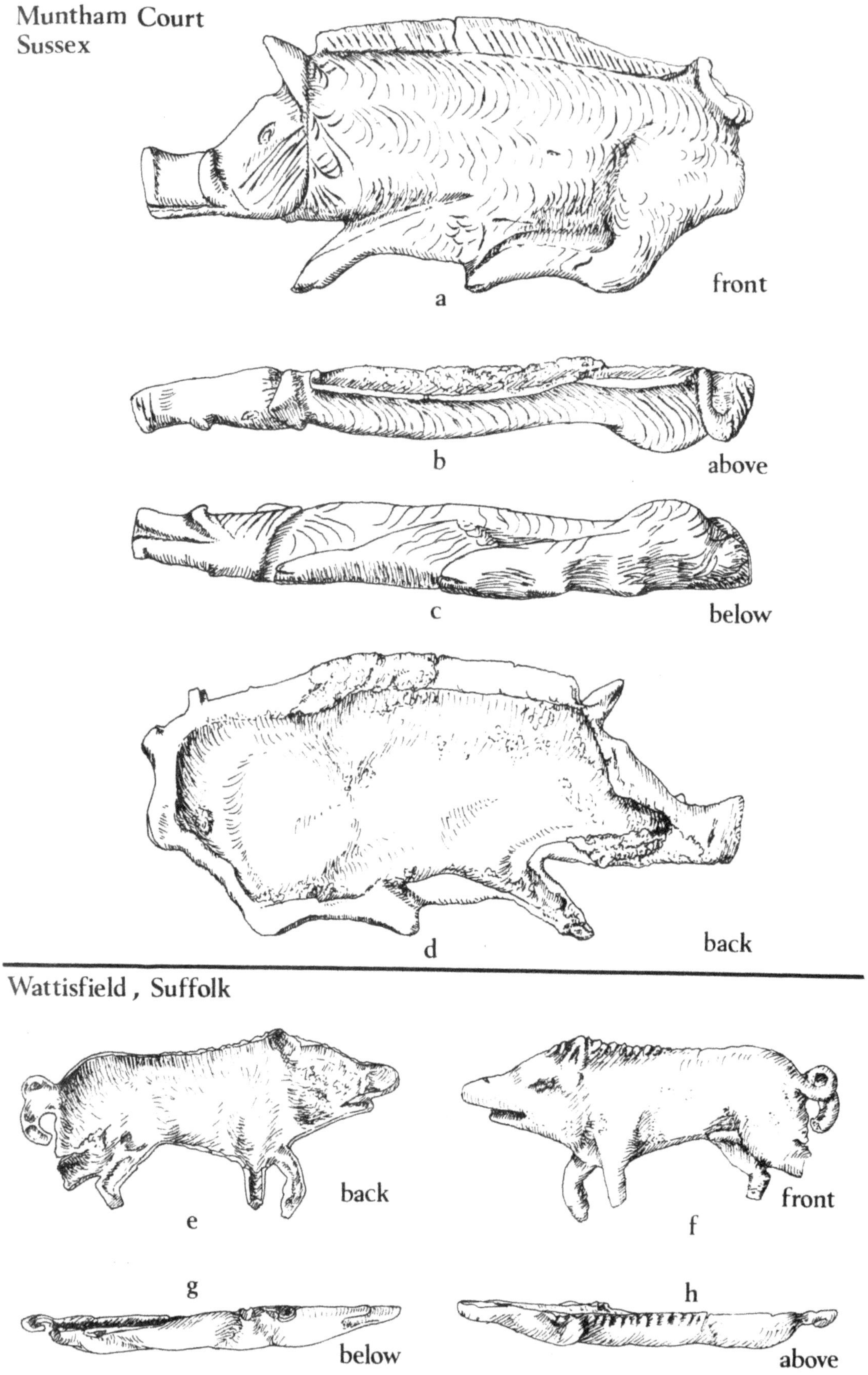

Muntham Court
Sussex

a front

b above

c below

d back

Wattisfield, Suffolk

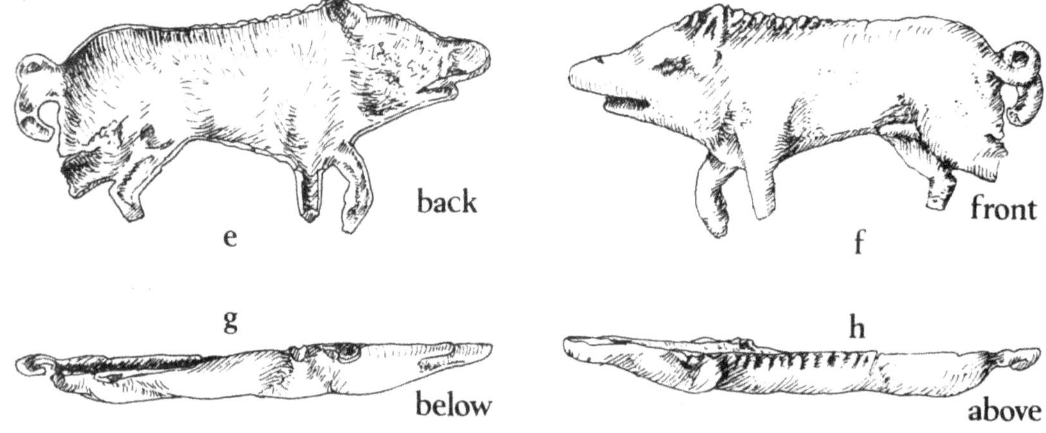

Fig. 9 Boar plaques from Muntham Court, Sussex and Wattisfield, Suffolk. Scale 1:1.

ents the remnant of Celtic religious practice, lingering on in the Roman period. If the boar was indeed a "cult animal of particular significance", (Ross, 1967:321) one might expect to find vestiges of the cult in the Roman period. However, as the evidence for a boar cult in Britain before the conquest is meagre at best, a votive interpretation for the boar might be stretching the imagination a little too far.

All the arguments concerning the Muntham Court plaque seem inconclusive. However, the 20th legion in Britain had the boar as its emblem and it is possible that several of the other Roman figures are examples of this (Parker, 1958). The boar symbol is widespread in the Roman period. There are for example a large number of clay antefixes showing in relief the figure of a running boar, the legionary standard and the letters LEG XX. These were produced specifically for the Twentieth legion at Holt, Denbighshire (Grimes, 1930) and have been found in large numbers at Chester (Deva) the headquarters of the Twentieth legion. Further evidence is furnished by a small bronze medallion showing the running boar, which was found during the current excavations at the legionary fortress of Usk, Monmouthshire. Dr. William Manning (personal communication) feels that the Twentieth legion is the one most likely to be associated with Usk, and that the medallion may therefore represent the emblem. It can be dated to an early military context, during the reign of Nero, or the very first years of Vespasian, i.e. mid-first century A.D.

Another of the boar figurines is associated with Chesters Roman Fort on Hadrian's Wall (Fig. 10). The obvious connection here with the army leads to the attractive proposal that this boar also is an emblem of the 20th Legion; this must however remain an unsubstantiated suggestion. Discussion about the function of this boar proves no more conclusive. It consists of a head only, and is obviously meant for attachment, being hollow. Like the boar from Aldborough (see below), it has a hole through the nose, but it is unlikely that this was intended for suspension, as the amount of wear on the edges of the hole, albeit obscured by corrosion, is incommensurate with this sort of treatment. It is possible, in the case of the Chesters head, that the hole was provided for tusks of some organic material, which have since decayed. There are no tusks cast on the figure, but the nose part is so badly corroded that it would be impossible now to analyse the residue for organic matter.

Dr. Morna Simpson (personal communication) has suggested that the Chesters head might be the end of a knife handle; the wear on the crest could be compatible with this. Examples of the same kind of object are known from Roman Britain, like the skillet with a dog's head on the handle from Canterbury, of the first or second century A.D. (Toynbee, 1964:127).

A similar boar's head was found as part of a hoard in 1857; it was ploughed up from a field called the Hempsalls in the parish of Willingham, Cambridgeshire. (Fig. 10). Like the Chesters boar, it is hollow and evidently designed as an attachment, though whether for a practical object like a knife is difficult to say. The head is very small and the horns might prove an inconvenience. If the other objects in the hoard can still be described as ritual, as in earlier discussions (Rostovtseff, 1923) the boar's head

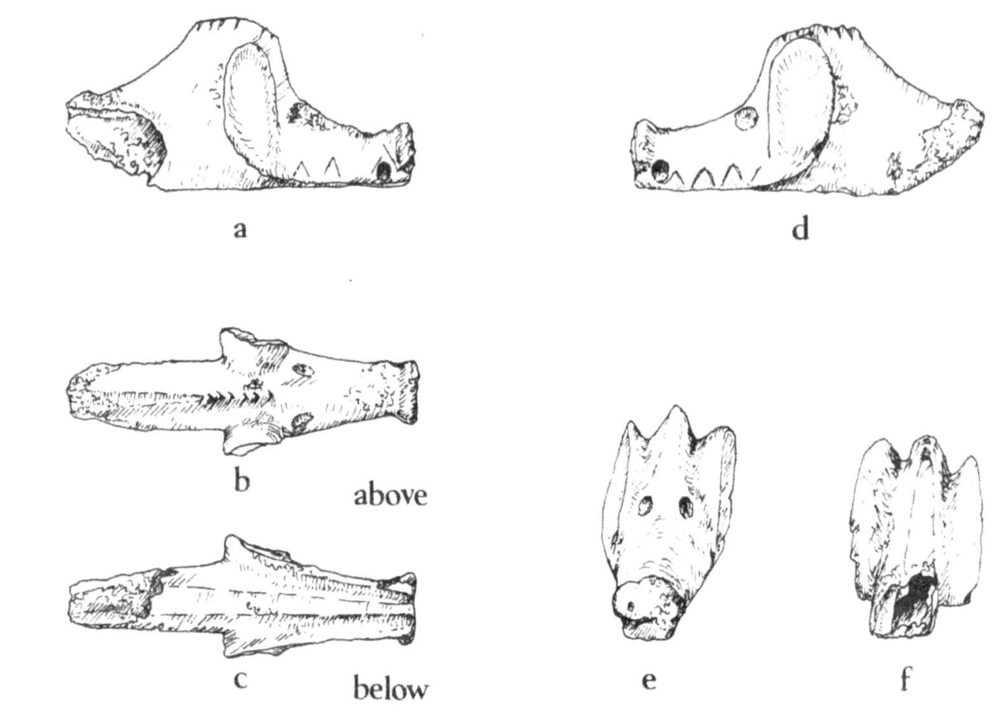

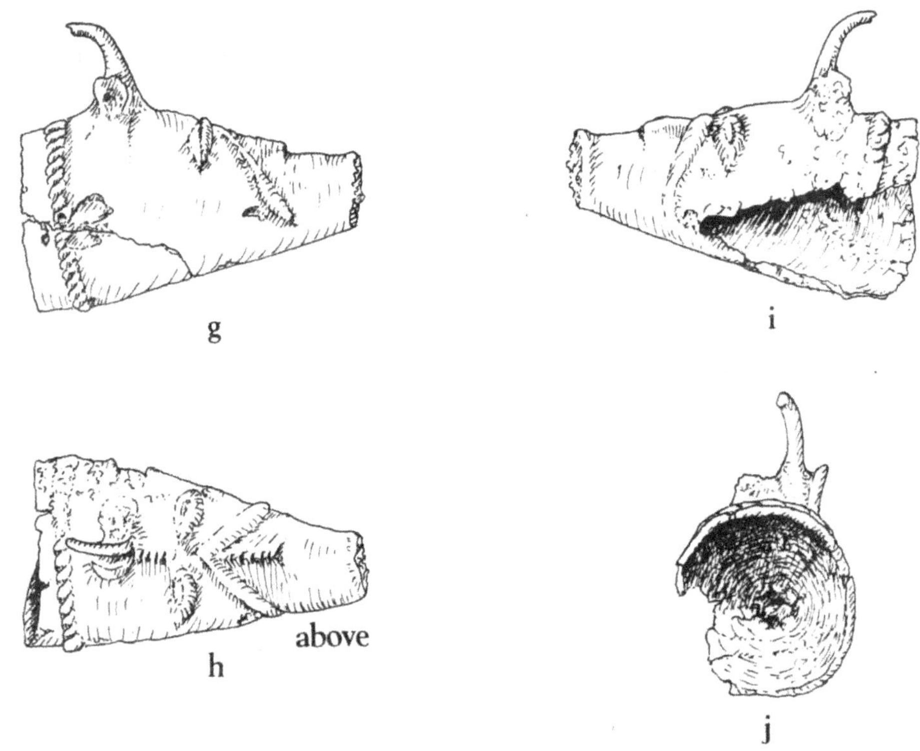

Fig. 10 Boar heads from Chesters, Northumberland and Willingham Fen, Cambs. Scale 1:1.

could alternatively be thought of as a cult object. Though the hoard is Roman in date, the 'sceptre' or club incorporates native concepts, with Tanaris (a local equation of Jupiter) clustered around the stem with his various symbols, a wheel, an eagle and a three-horned bull. The date of the group seems to rest on the identification of the emperor whose portrait adorns the top of the sceptre; he is usually said to be Antoninus Pius (Toynbee, 1964:53), or Commodus (Rostovtseff, 1923:92) i.e. 138-161 A.D. or 176-192 A.D. All the objects including the boar are native in style and crudely designed, so much so that when published by Rostovtseff in 1923, the boar's head was described as that of a bull. (see also Toynbee, 1964:124). Nevertheless it has characteristics similar to those of the other boar figurines, notably snout and tusks. What makes the identification doubtful is the horn issuing from between the ears, possibly one of a pair; the ridge running up the nose; and the torc or rope around its neck. Perhaps this figure was an imaginary composite creature, similar to the three horned bulls of Gaul (Wheeler, 1943:75f), one of which appears on the sceptre from Willingham Fen.

There are three boar figurines that must be grouped together because of their similarity; these are the boar foreparts from Aldborough, Yorkshire (a Roman town); Eastcheap; and " London" now in the Sydney Museum. (Fig. 11, and plates X and XI). They are all cast in the same way, with forelegs thrust well forward, a projecting hind part and a hole through the nose. Signs of wear on the nose, and filing, especially between the legs, are clear on all the figures. Megaw (1969) felt that all three were Roman in date, although the Nicholson boar (Sydney) "of comparatively late date, is wholly native in feeling". (1969:46). I would agree that the two London boars are provincial rather than Roman in style, although that from Aldborough shows more naturalism. There is really little to suggest a definite date for any of these objects and the problem may only be solved by a quantitative analysis of their metal content. As to their function, Megaw suggests that they were designed as fittings, perhaps attached to the rim of a cup or vessel, the hole being for a suspension ring. The legs and belly of the Eastcheap boar subtend an almost exact right angle as though it were designed to fit onto a metal or wooden object, which might support this theory.

From the point of view of style, the sophisticated boar from Colchester (Fig. 12) should probably be considered Roman. Its context is said to be Colchester, but its early discovery (before 1863; Pollexfen, 1863) gives one little confidence as to the accuracy of the information. There can be no doubt that this is a figure of a boar, a splendid animal and beautifully modelled, of which Toynbee's comment - "a complete figure of the beast... rough, but naturalistic in treatment," hardly does justice. (1964:125). One interesting feature of this boar is that the left side is extremely worn, presumably as the result of contact during its period of use. There is little more that can be said of this boar; its function can hardly be conjectured although it is obviously freestanding. There is no evidence of fixtures in its cloven feet, the bases of which are completely smooth.

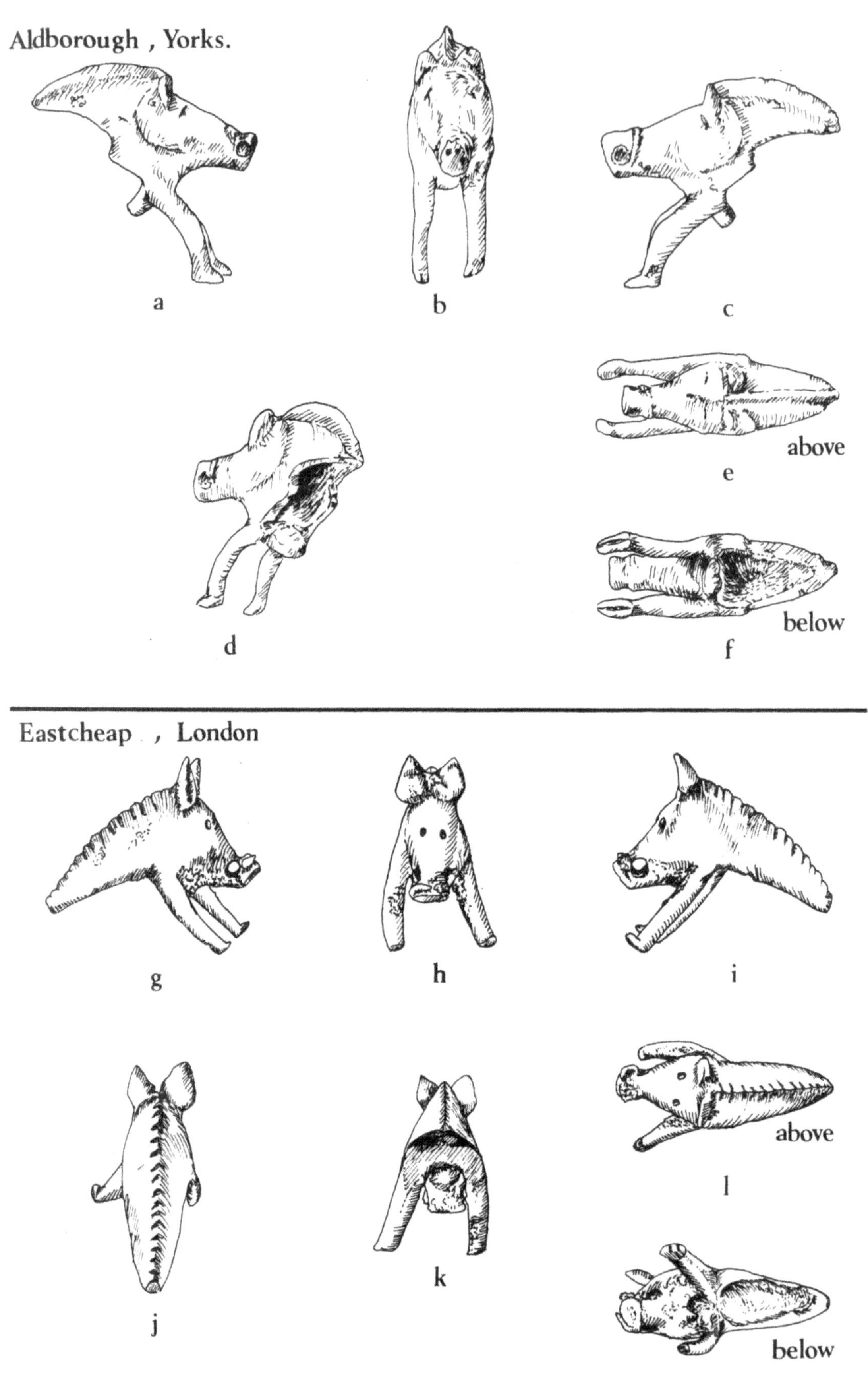

Fig. 11 Boar foreparts from Aldborough, Yorks. and Eastcheap, London. Scale 1:1.

BOARS OF UNCERTAIN DATE OR PROVENANCE

There are three other boars which deserve mention, although little is known of them. One is known only as a vague reference in the Victoria County History of Warwickshire; it was found with some samian pottery and several Roman coins, in the parish of Weston-on-Avon, Warwickshire. (Doubleday and Page, 1904:249). These finds were published in 1866, but no trace is left of the boar, and since the Warwickshire County Museum have no record of this object, it must be regarded as lost.

The other two figurines are in the National Museum of Ireland, Dublin. (Plates XII and XIII). They are of unknown provenance, in fact Richard Haworth suggests (private communication) that they should not definitely be regarded as coming from Ireland. Both are beautifully modelled with hatching as decoration across their flanks and one has hooked back feet as though designed to be attached to some other object. They are not, however, as asserted by Francoise Henry, (1940, Pl. 4C), figures of wild boars; one at least is a sow, the other is obviously male, and probably both are representations of domestic pigs. The lack of tusks, the small crest and ears, short legs and stocky body, and snout-like nose, all point to domestication. In this case they are unlikely to date from much before the Roman Conquest of Britain, and could conceivably be Medieval, although their similarity to the boar on the Mérida Chariot (Megaw, 1970 No. 37), might preclude this suggestion. Again any theory as to their useful function would owe much to an active imagination.

ANGLO-SAXON BOARS

Not included in this review of the British figurines are two boars of Anglo-Saxon date, which have been adequately published elsewhere. That on a helmet from Benty Grange, Derbyshire (Bruce-Mitford, 1974:223f) is from a tumulus grave of the pagan Saxon period. Very similar in shape, and from a grave context, is the bronze figurine from Guilden Morden, Cambridgeshire, hitherto as "Celtic" (Fordham, 1904) and in the Prehistoric Catalogue of the British Museum. (Brailsford, 1953). The objects found with the boar mark it as Saxon; it has been duly published as such (Foster, 1977) and been transferred to the Department of Medieval and Later Antiquities at the British Museum.

REPRESENTATION

In concluding this description of the figurines, it is pertinent to the discussion to ask whether they actually represent boars. The Chesters head, for example, with its lack of tusks, upturned nose and squashed high face, is suspiciously reminiscent of a domesticated pig. The Muntham Court figurine has an upturned curly tail, which would be held by Bokonyi (1974:215) to be proof of domestication, although the figure as a whole looks wild. Where the crest is emphasised and the snout enlongated rather than rounded, the artist has probably intended to portray a boar. In the case of the Lexden and Colchester figurines, there can scarcely be any doubt, but with the re-

Colchester , Essex

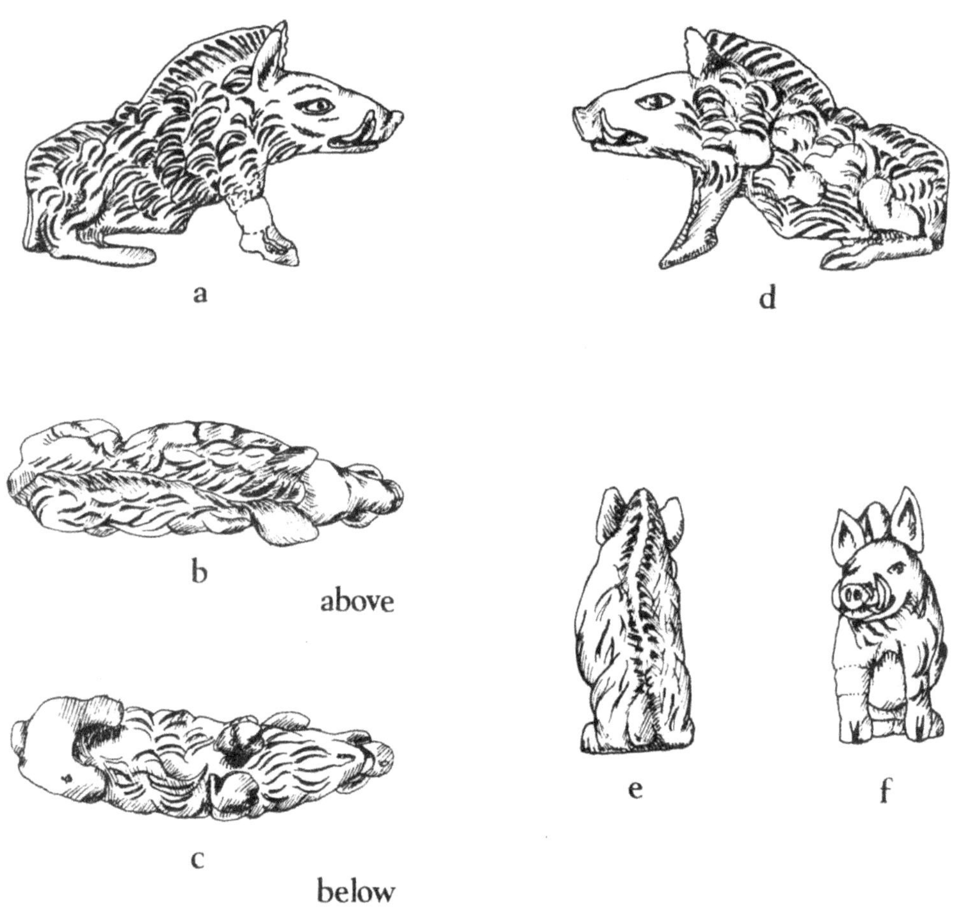

Fig. 12 Seated boar figurine from Colchester, Essex. Scale 1:1.

mainder, we come up against the problem of domestication of the pig in prehistoric Europe. Although little has been written on this subject, it seems likely that pigs were allowed to run semi-wild in the deciduous forests and to mate with wild stock. This assumption accords with Strabo's comment (Tierney, 1960:268) concerning the Celts, "Their pigs are allowed to run wild and are noted for their height, and pugnacity and swiftness. It is dangerous for a stranger to approach them, and also for a wolf". If this were the case, representations of domesticated pigs might appear wild to our unaccustomed eyes. On reflection the connection of these figurines with the "supreme cult animal of the Celts" (Ross, 1967:321) becomes less and less evident. I find it difficult to understand how anyone could extend this description to the boar from Woodingdean, which Leeds was pleased to call a "pert little beast". (1933:95).

CONCLUSION

Considering the number of animal figurines in Britain, it is surprising that so little is known of their function. Of the twenty-two bronze boars known to the author only four show obvious signs of attachment, and these are unlikely to be helmet crests, as supposed by a number of authors. Liversidge (1968:147) has proposed that a number of the freestanding animal figurines may have been toys. She suggests that a bronze mouse from a child's grave in Roman York is too appealing to have religious or votive significance. But because the function of many of the boar figurines appears elusive, they have often been regarded as votive offerings. For example, the Sussex boars were referred to in the Brighton Herald (Toms, 1918:4) thus: "The small ornaments in question might have had a totemic meaning, or they might have constituted the first 'lucky pigs' on record". Megaw (1970:19) sees the boar as "one of the most potent forms in the Celtic mythological zoo". Ross gives them a purely religious interpretation, seeming to regard all boar representations as evidence of the Celtic and heroic world, symbolic of "the passions of the Celtic peoples - hunting, feasting, fighting, and procreation." (1968:321). This is surely dangerous. Certainly the Irish Celtic writings contain myths concerning mystical boar hunts and feasts, (Rees and Rees, 1961) and some of the boar figurines in Britain may reflect these myths, but how many? I have already conjectured that some of the boars may be emblems of the Twentieth legion, and others may be, as Toynbee suggests (1964:125) offerings by hunters. This is not to suggest that a votive interpretation is wrong, merely that it is unsubstantiated. At the same time however, I wholly agree with Thomas (1961:39) when he denies that the animals of Celtic art were used only to relieve unadorned surfaces - "They seldom served merely as ornaments. Each creature possessed obvious virtues, its own peculiar and widespread mana: the wild boar with its lack of fear, dangerous tusks and thick coarse-haired skin was an obvious choice to adorn a warrior's shield or war-horn; ... when we consider that, from an early stage in almost all historically-documented societies, these virtues and special properties were generally expressed in terms of pantheistic religion, we have the real clue to the retention of animal style art."

Throughout this discussion, references to a number of authors make it clear that central to the problem of interpretation is the extent to which the figurines can be considered Celtic. Ross (1967) looks upon the Celts as a group bound by linguistic and ethnic ties, implying a common cultural heritage. Some apply the term primarily to a particular art style of which the Hounslow boars are the only boar representatives in Britain. The term used in this limited sense has little validity, for it poses the question as to whether the boars made in the same context and yet in a different style can be called Celtic. Piggott (1965) uses the term to imply an economic and political unity in La Tène Europe. He emphasises the unity in particular, the Celtic tribes forming a trading network with a continual flow of finished goods and raw materials. "A map of the often noble ox-headed iron fire-dogs or of a standardised type of jointed rod-and-chain hanger for a cauldron over an open fire for instance, shows a Common Market area from Britain to Czechoslovakia and Austria". (1965:247). Interchange between the civilised and "barbarian" world took place constantly, and material evidence reveals that products of the Roman world were eagerly obtained by the natives of northern Europe. (Cf. Peacock, 1971).

This reciprocation is held to extend beyond economics, to art, metal-working traditions and perhaps even to religion. On the basis of such a broad definition, the Iron Age boar figurines would be regarded as part of a common Celtic tradition, and this despite the fact that few show characteristics typical of the Celtic art style.

I am unwilling to argue that the presence of boars in Roman and post-Roman Britain indicates a continuity of Celtic tradition. We have seen above (Page 5) that the boar plays an inconsiderable part in the Roman array of animal figurines. Even if the I on Age boars do reflect Celtic mythology and the sacred boar hunt (Rees and Rees, 1961 ; 70), this interpretation can scarcely be applied to late-Roman representations. There is, for example, a silver gilt fibula from Sussex, now in the British Museum (Frend, 1955:17) which has a very Celtic-looking boar's head on the bow, and a chi rho symbol (☧) on the catch plate. The association of a Celtic deity (if such it is) with a Christian symbol in such a context cannot surely be a conscious act. There were in any case a number of other barbarian traditions extant in Europe during the Roman period, some of which venerated the boar. The Scandinavian pre-Christian myths, for example, include stories of a god Frey, whose symbol was a boar. Even after the Christian conversions, the literature contains numerous references to boars and to boar-capped helmets. Beowulf has five instances (Beowulf, 1968, pp 40, 63, 68, 72 and 94). The Anglo-Saxon boar figurines from Britain, from Guilden Morden and Benty Grange, may represent a Germanic tradition re-introduced from Europe in the post-Roman period, rather than a legacy of Celtic myth surviving the 400 plus years of Roman civilising influence. Toynbee herself admitted that "the direct artistic legacy of Roman art to Anglo-Saxon England was extremely slight". (1964:442).

However, despite my remarks above, it is obvious from recent studies of post conquest Britain that a great deal of Iron Age tradition survived into the Roman period. It is clear that the earlier writers exaggerated the degree of Romanising influence and that many parts of Britain received only a superficial change in the pattern of subsistence.

"The traditional view that the coming of Rome, military and ecclesiastic, acted as a kind of guillotine lopping off clearly and decisively the native element in Britain is fortunately being greatly modified" (Ross, 1967:5). Rivet in particular, (1958) stresses the need to regard British history as a continuous sequence, and recent excavations, e.g. at Lockleys, Herts., and Horndean, Hants (Cunliffe, 1961) have shown continuity of settlement in which exploitation of the surrounding farmland was obviously unchanged by the Roman intrusion, even if the architecture of the farm house altered. Iron

Age economy and way of life was not destroyed as the result of the Roman Conquest. Jope (1961) and Toynbee (1964) have both shown the survival of the Celtic art style into the Roman period, and Ross (1967) discusses the survival of the cult of the head, which despite its barbaric connotations, is very much in evidence on Roman archaeological sites. It is difficult to know, however, how relevant this general feeling of traditional continuity is to the small number of figurines forming the basis of the present discussion. If they can be given a religious interpretation, it is of consequence that interest in the boar survives into the Roman period. But it appears that only occasionally is a religious or votive interpretation justified; in other cases it cannot be substantiated. The perennial problem inevitably creeps in, that it is unsatisfactory to base elaborate arguments on unassociated and undateable objects.

CATALOGUE OF BRITISH BOAR FIGURINES

1. Meare Lake Village, Somerset (Fig. 2, Plate I)

Length 64 mm; Height 34 mm.

Face broken off, obviously originally hollow or pierced, and appears to have had an iron core (Stippled on Fig. 1.). Groove along back to take a crest of bronze. Condition fairly good, but crest degraded.

Ref: Bulleid and Gray, 1953:222f. Said to have been found on 2nd floor of Mound XV at Meare West Lake Village in 1913.

Probably Iron Age in date: c. third century B.C. - first century A.D.

Somerset County Museum; E53.

2. Lexden Tumulus, near Colchester, Essex (Figs. 3 and 4, Plate II).

Length 85 mm; Height 70 mm.

Roman in style; bad condition - all feet broken off, and badly scarred surface. Now restored and active bronze disease halted. Although worn, the surface shows pieces of bronze inset, a bronze-working technique "Flicken-Reparabuten", well-known on classical bronzes.

Ref: Laver, 1927:241-254, Fig. 4, and Foster, in preparation. Found during excavation of Tumulus by Laver. Associations include bronze bull; table; altar; studs; silver medallion c. 17 B.C., of Augustus; amphorae.

Colchester and Essex Museum. No accession number.

3. Hounslow, Middlesex, Hoard B (Fig. 5, plate IIIA).

A. Length 46 mm; Height 30 mm; Stand 12 mm x 9 mm at widest.

Condition good, but stand only partially complete, and tusks corroded. Found in a field by labourers, 1864; associated with boars B and C, two indeterminate animals and a bronze wheel.

Ref: Franks, 1864:90.

British Museum; 64.5 - 1.9 Given 1864.

4. B. Length 78 mm; Height 45 mm. (Fig. 5, Plate IIIB).

Freestanding boar in good condition, but a large amount of surface corrosion; crest, once openwork is now broken, found with Hounslow A, 1864.

British Museum; 64.5 - 1.8

5. C. Length, 70 mm; Height, 50 mm. (Fig. 6 a-e, Plate IIIC).

Openwork crest with punched holes, now broken; filing marks on left flank. Condition good except left foreleg and tail (broken) and earlier corrosion covering most of face.

Found with Hounslow A, 1864.

British Museum; 64.5.2.17.

6. Woodingdean (Woodendean), Happy Valley, Brighton, Sussex (Fig. 6 f-l, Plate V).

Length, 33 mm; Height, 24 mm.

Freestanding boar with accentuated crest, no tusks or mouth shown. Eyes appear to be stamped. Condition good, except crest is worn. Found in 1905 during gravel digging.

Ref. Toms, 1907:271. Appears to be associated with swan's neck pin.

Brighton Museum.

7. Kemp Town, Brighton, Sussex

Size is said to be similar to that of boar from Woodingdean.

Ref. Toms, 1907:489-90; 1918:4. Dug up by Mr. W. Walton of Bennet Road, Kemp Town, during excavations in the ten years before 1918. Associated with a 3rd century B.C. brooch. Boar lost soon after discovery.

8. East Sussex, Barbican House Museum, Lewes. (Fig. 7 a-f, Plate VIa & b).

Length, 36 mm; Height 19 mm.

Very few details remain due to extensive corrosion. Crude animal with a pronounced crest. Right hind leg is broken.

Ref. Toms, 1907:271. Circumstances of discovery unknown.

Lewes Castle Museum.

9. East London. (Fig. 7, g-l, Plate VIc).

Length 41 mm; Height, 26 mm.

Crude design similar to previous entry, prominent crest. Condition bad with extensive corrosion especially on face, and no original details visible. Right foreleg and left ear are broken.

Ref. Vulliamy, 1930:134.

Found before 1865 by Roach Smith in "East London".

British Museum, Roach Smith Collection. 56.7-1.21.

10. Gower Peninsula, Rhossilly, Glamorganshire. (Fig. 8 a-f, Plate IVa).

Length, 56 mm; Height, 25 mm max.

Crude, freestanding boar, legs totally without features, and very worn. Condition fairly good, with stabilised bronze disease.

Ref: Gray and Bulleid, 1953:224. Ashmolean Visitors Report, 1936, part II, 16.

Circumstances of discovery unknown.

Ashmolean Museum, 1936:175.

11. Gaer Fawr (Guilsfield Without), Montgomeryshire. (Fig. 8 g-l, Plate IV b & c).

Length, 63 mm; Height, 35 mm.

Crude figure, hollow bronze, with deep incision running the full length underneath the belly. Surface very worn and corroded, little of the original surface remaining.

Ref. Barnwell, 1871:163-7, Fig. P. 163. R.C.H.M. Montgomery, 1911: 46, Fig. 13.

National Museum of Wales; 70 35H.

12. Muntham Court, Findon, Sussex. (Fig. 9 a-d, Plate VII a & b).

Length, 40 mm; Height, 45 mm.

Plaque of a charging boar, hollow behind, but with no visible means of attachment. Condition good, though surface is slightly worn.

Ref: Burstow and Holleyman 1958:170.

Found in the forecourt of a Romano-Celtic shrine, with other Romano-British objects.

Worthing Museum, given by excavators, 1956.

13. Wattisfield, Suffolk. (Fig. 9 e-h, Plate VII c and d).

Length, 65 mm; Max. Height, 30 mm.

Very shallow plaque of a male pig. Sex clearly shown, but no tusks, only a small crest and ears, and curly tail - all indicating domestication. Few surface details remain due to intense wear. Front hind leg is broken due to corrosion.

Ref: Moore, 1947; 166-8: Fig. 5.

Found in 1943 in a land draining operation, in a field adjoining Foxledge Common, Suffolk.

Ipswich County Museum, 1945:116.

14. Chesters Roman Fort, Hadrians Wall, Northumberland. (Fig. 10 a-f, Plate IX a and b).

Length, 46 mm; Height, 23 mm.

Boar's head only, hollow, with hole through nose. Very active bronze disease and corrosion; also fairly worn. Shape suggests domestication. Engraved details on each side of face, on the jowls.

Ref.: Wallis Budge, 1903:385.

Chesters Fort Museum, 3085.

15. Willingham Fen, Cambridgeshire. (Fig. 10 g-j, Plate IXc).

Length, 48 mm; Height, 37 mm.

Boar's head only, hollow, with moulded eyes and tusks, and a torc or rope around neck. One ear and perhaps one horn broken off.

Ref.: Rostovtseff, 1923:92.

Found in 1857, part of a hoard.

Cambridge Museum of Archaeology and Ethnography, 15185a.

16. Aldborough, Yorkshire. (Fig. 11 a-f, Plate XI a and b).

Length, 40 mm; Height, 35 mm.

Head, back and forelegs only of a boar, with a knob for attachment between legs and a hole through the nose. Hollow behind. Note that the boar is slightly different from 1854 engraving.

Ref.: Smith, 1854, Pl. 25, Fig. 16.

Aldborough Museum, no accession number.

17. Eastcheap, London (Fig. 11 g-m, Plate XI c and d).

Length, 37 mm; Height, 34 mm.

Head, back and forelegs only, with a hole through the nose. Back and legs form a right angle. Condition fairly good, slight corrosion.

Ref.: Toms, 1907:490. Megaw, 1969:45-47, Plate 3.

Said to come from Eastcheap; associated with a tiny bronze mask, almost indecipherable, but perhaps an ox. Probably Roman in date.

London Museum, A2403. Purchased as part of the F. G. Hilton Collection.

18. London (Plate X).

35 mm, snout to rear.

Head, back and forelegs only, with a hole through the nose.

Ref.: Megaw, 1969:45-57, Plate 3.

Nicholson Museum, Sydney, Australia, R.489.

19. Colchester, Essex (Fig. 12, Plate XIe).

Length, 51 mm; Height, 33 mm.

Clearly a boar figurine, Roman in style; fur particularly clearly shown. Victorian pin in hind legs and right foreleg for mounting on a woodblock. Wear on left side is extensive; right leg is broken and restored.

Ref.: Pollexfen, 1863:508-10, Pl. XXIV, 9.

J. H. Pollexfen Collection, British Museum; purchased 1870.

20. Weston-on-Avon, Warwickshire

Bronze boar, small.

Ref.: Doubleday and Page, 1904:249.

Present location unknown.

21. Dublin (W11). (Plate XII and Plate XIIIa).

Approx. 82 mm long, 53 mm high.

Male pig covered with hatching to simulate hair; very small crest and small tusks. Back legs are bent forward at an awkward angle, and cloven. The right foreleg is broken.

Ref.: Armstrong, 1923:29 and Fig. 14.

National Museum of Ireland, Dublin; W11.

22. Dublin (W10). (Plate XIIIb).

Approximately same size as W11 (previous entry).

Bronze figure of a sow, with no tusks and a very small crest. Left back leg is broken, and some corrosion, but condition generally good.

Ref.: Armstrong, 1923:29 and Fig. 14.

National Museum of Ireland, Dublin; W10.

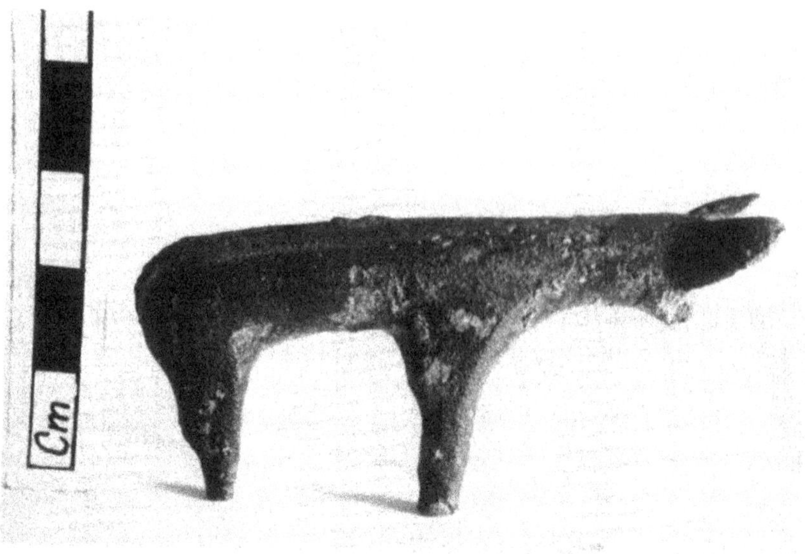

a

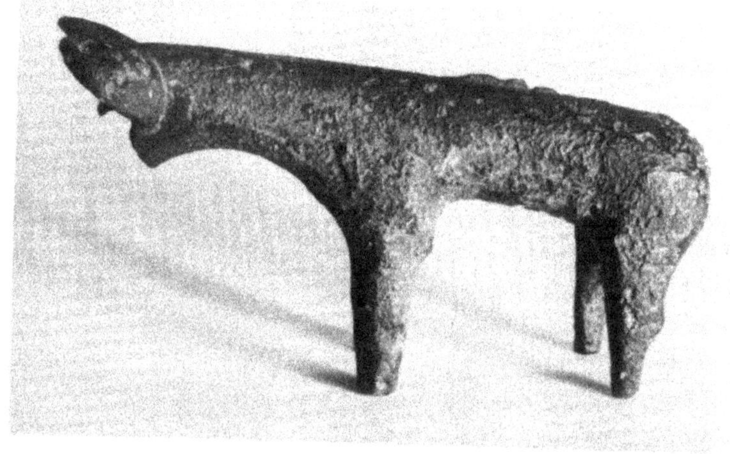

b

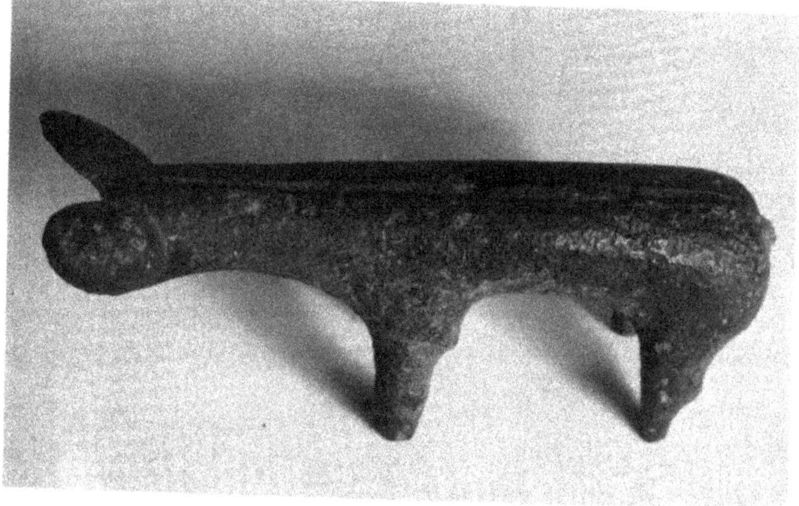

c

Plate I Boar figurine from Meare, Somerset. c: Top view showing groove along back.

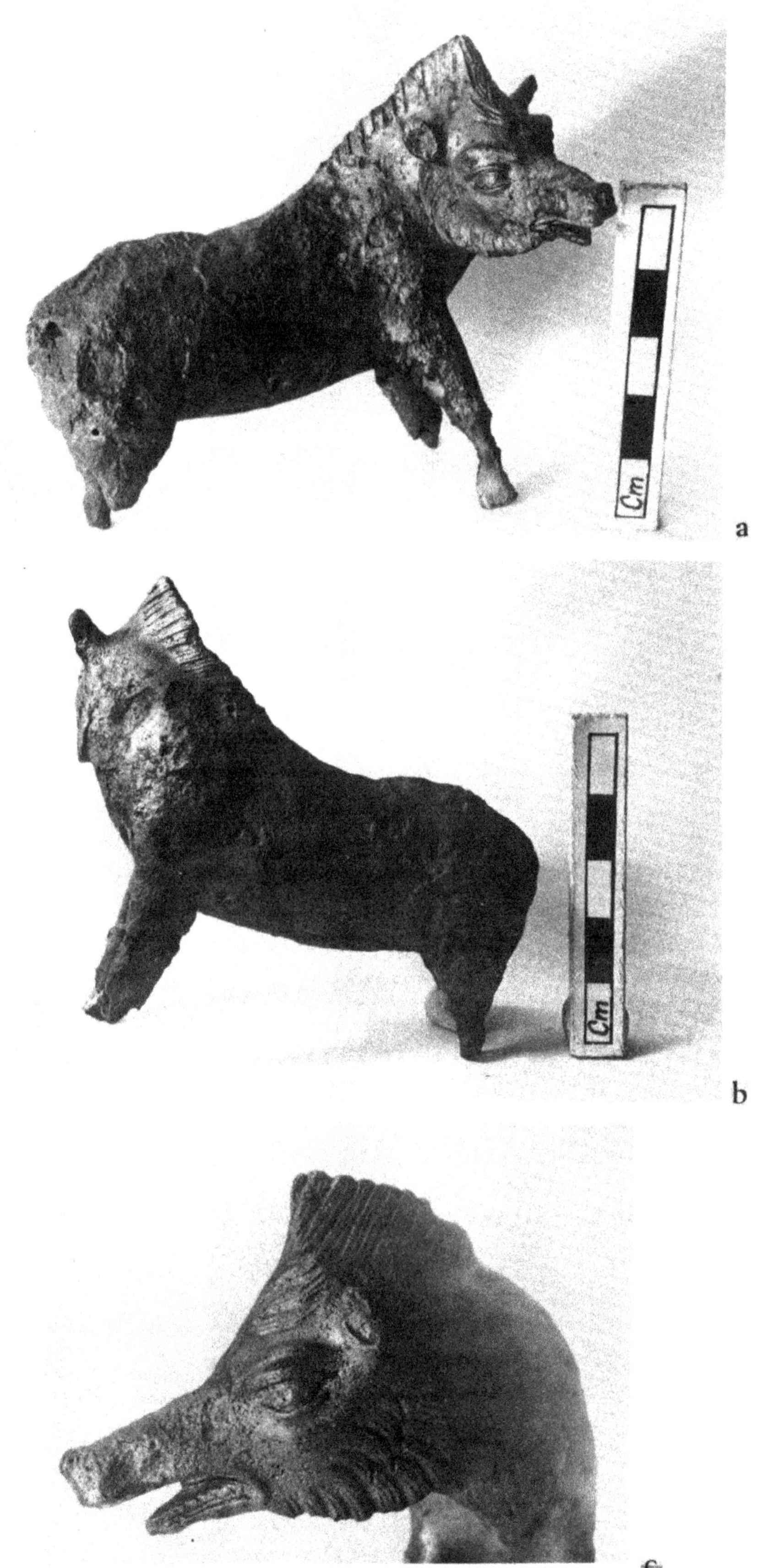

Plate II Boar figurine from Lexden Tumulus, Essex. c: Detail of face.

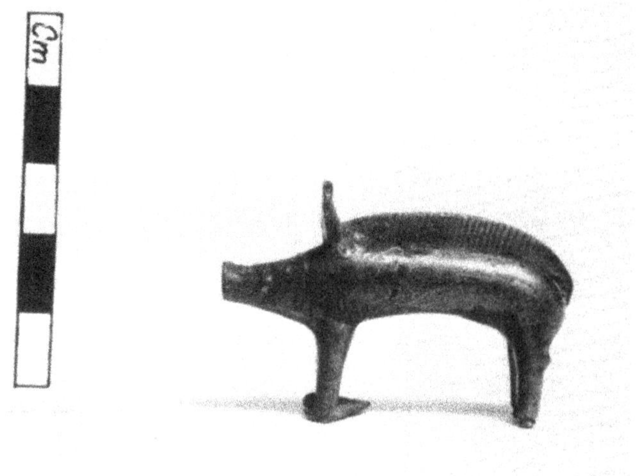

A

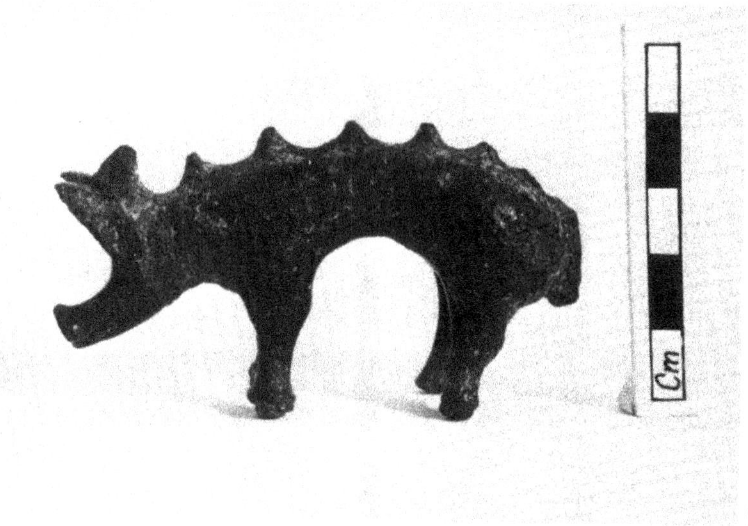

B

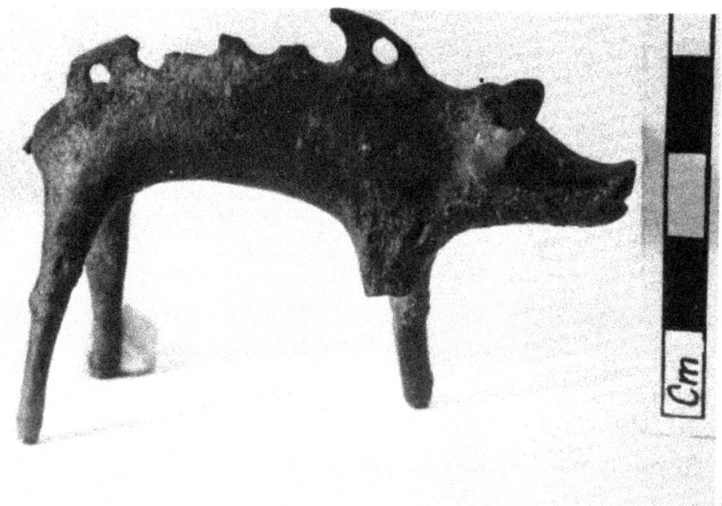

C

Plate III Boar figurines A, B, and C from Hounslow, Middlesex.

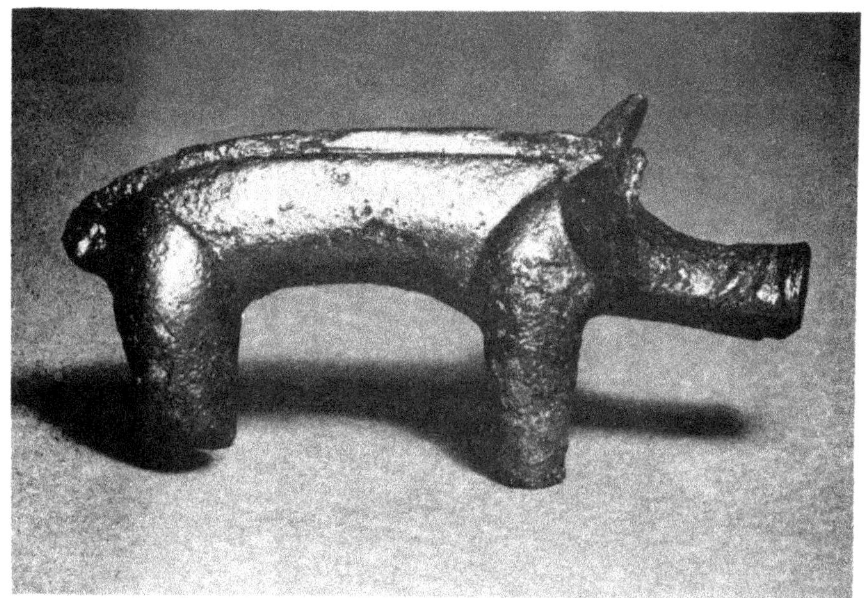

a

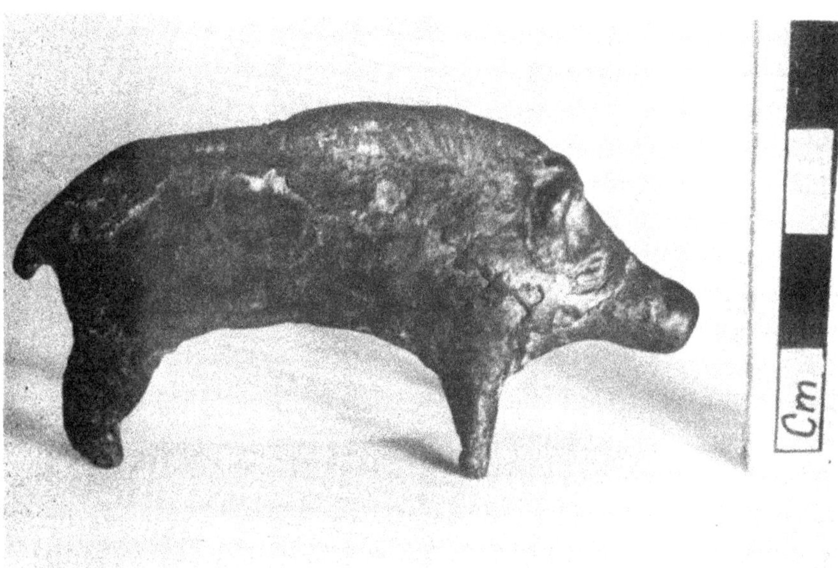

b

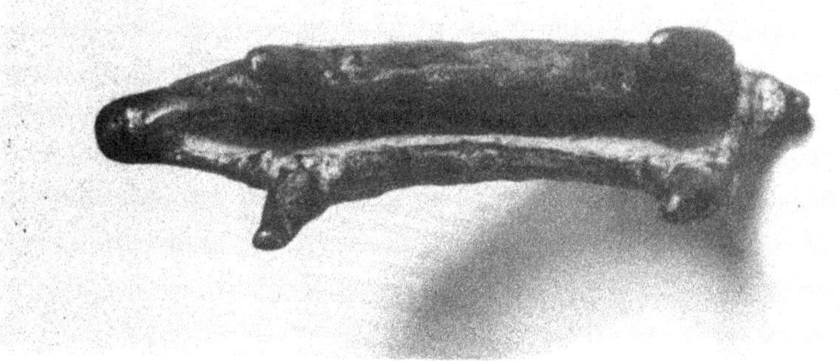

c

Plate IV Boar figurines from Gower peninsula, Glamorganshire (a) and Gaer Fawr, Montgomeryshire (b and c). c: View of Gaer Fawr boar from below, showing groove.

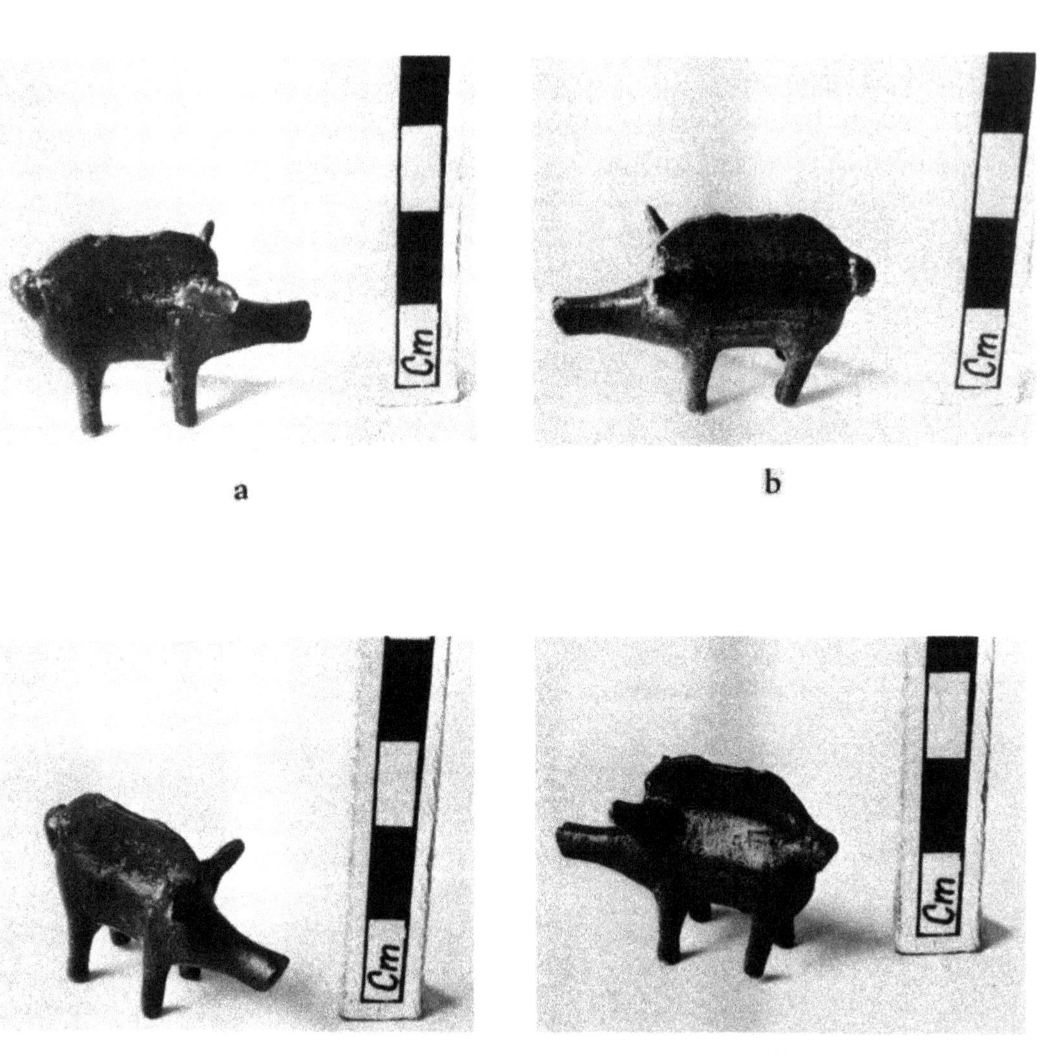

a

b

c

d

Plate V Boar figurine from Woodingdean, Sussex.

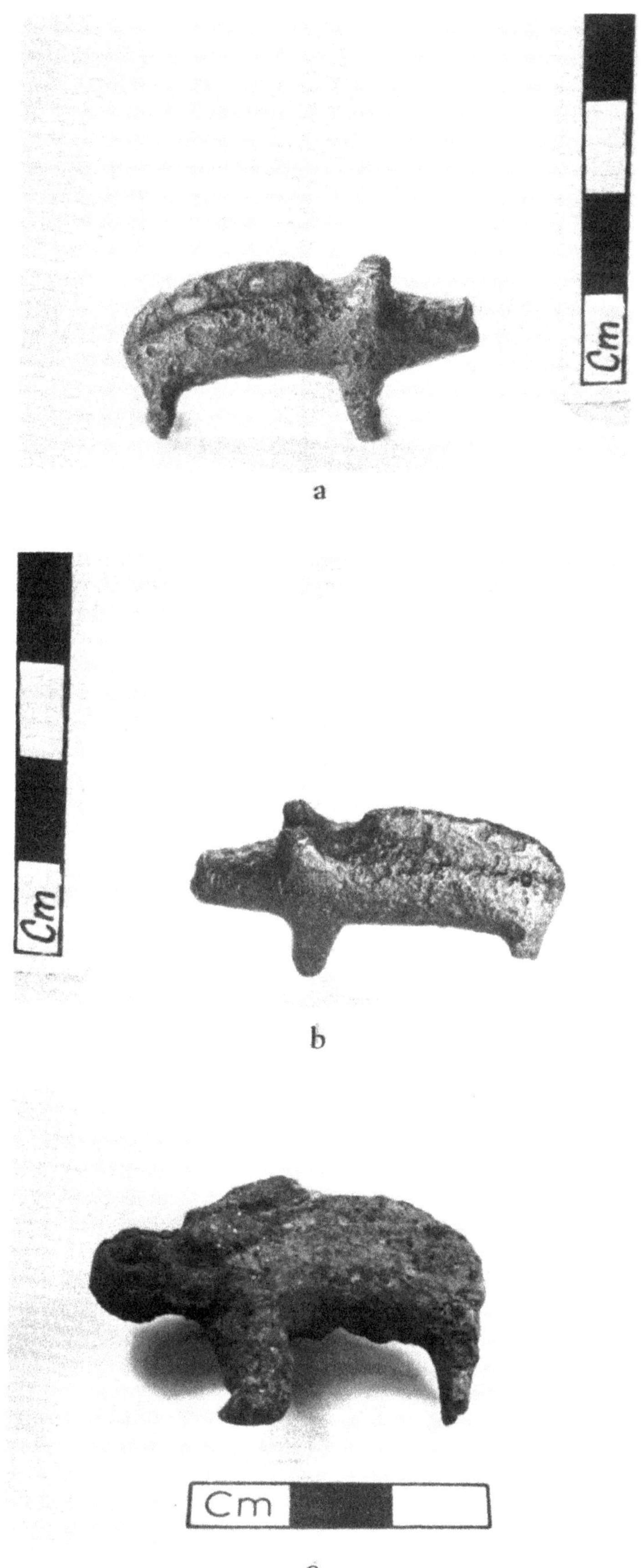

Plate VI Boar figurines from East Sussex (a and b) and East London (c).

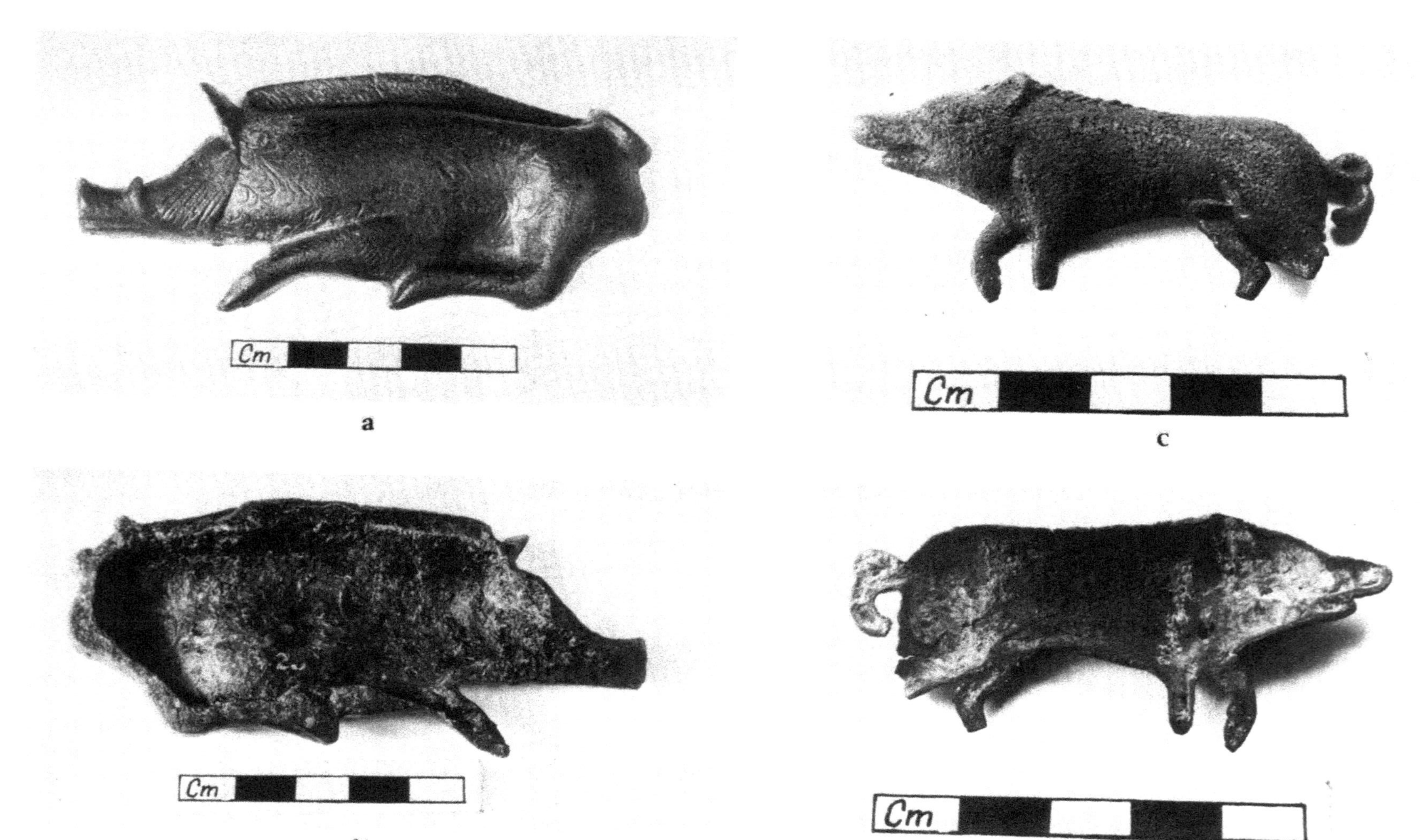

Plate VII Boar plaques from Muntham Court, Sussex (a: front, b: back) and Wattisfield, Suffolk (c: front, d: back).

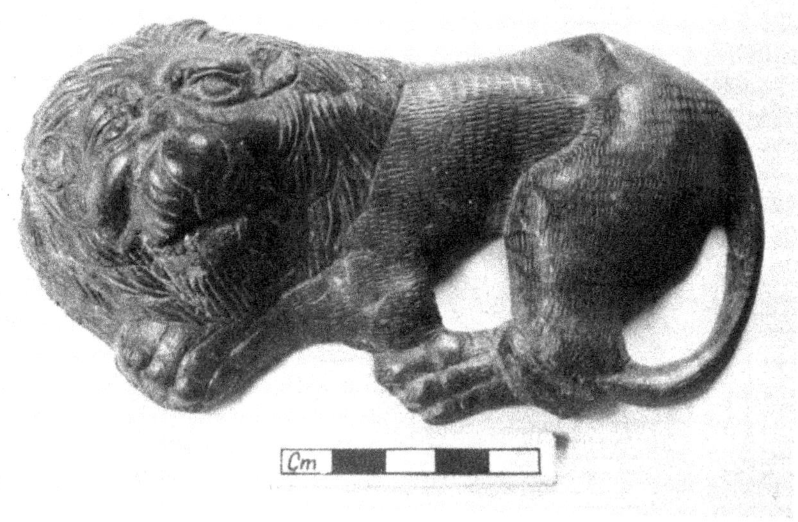

a

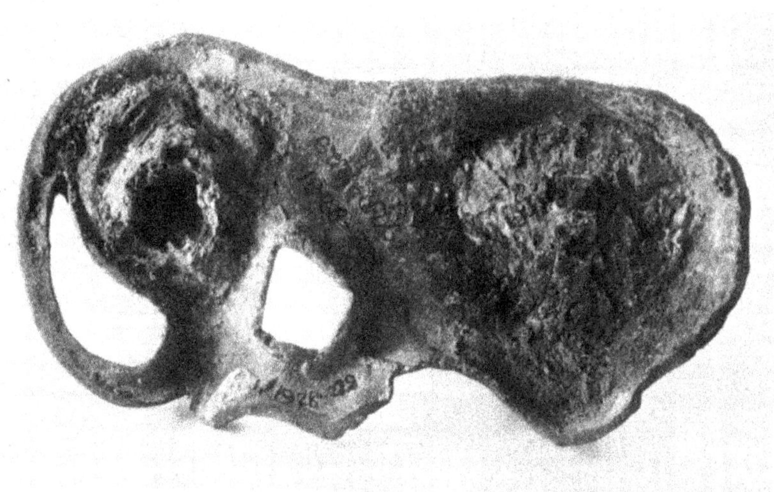

b

Plate VIII Lion plaque from Capel St. Mary, Suffolk. b: back view showing hollow back and iron rivets.

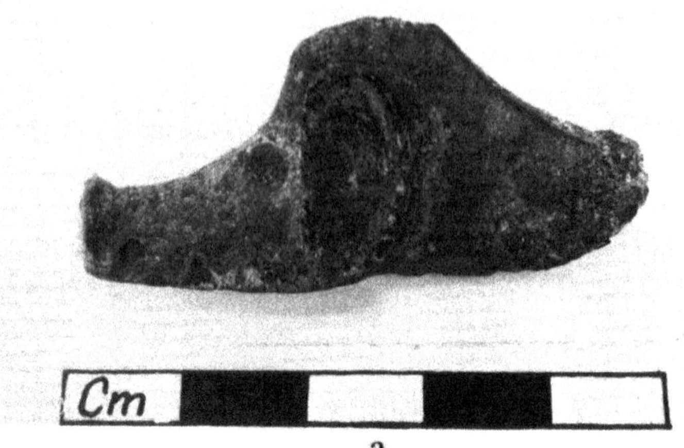

a

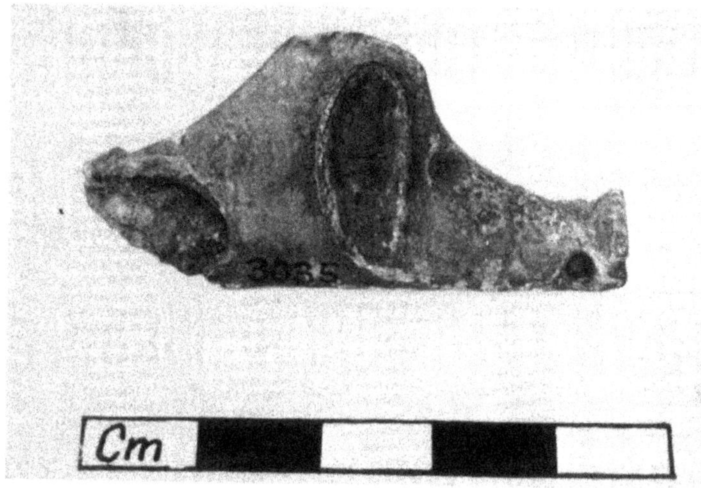

b

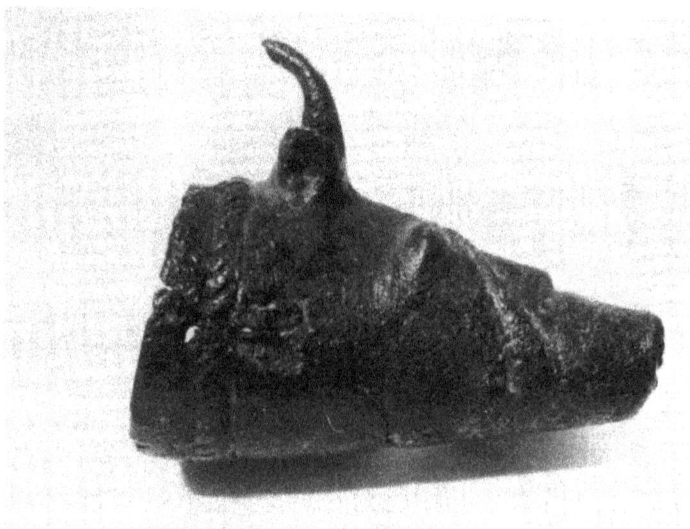

c

Plate IX Boar heads from Chesters, Northumberland (a and b) and Willingham Fen, Cambs. (c).

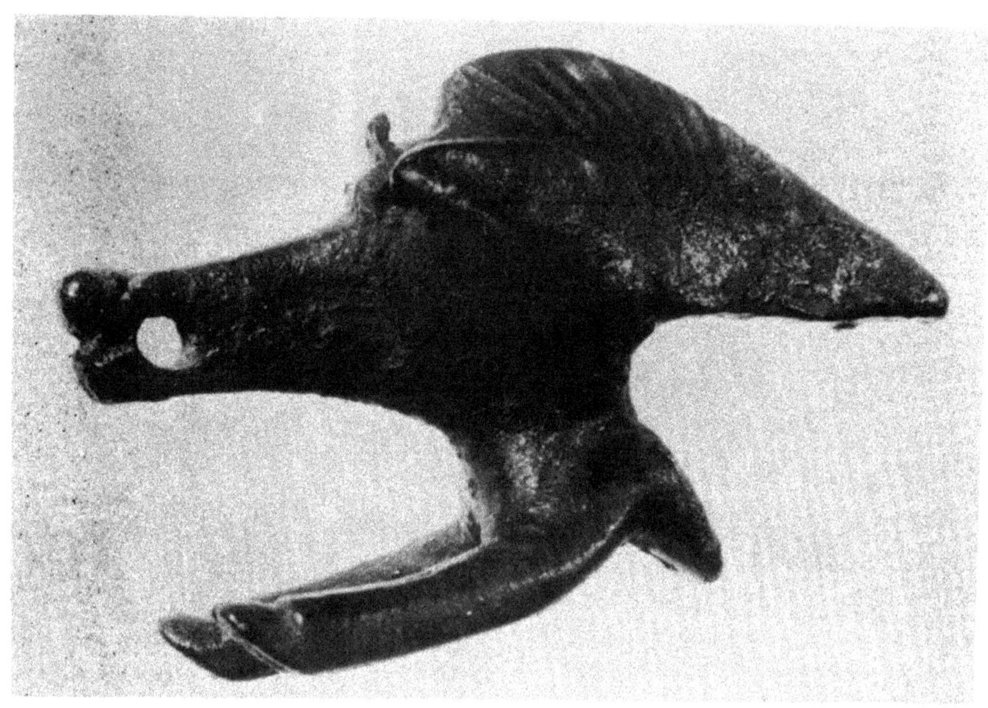

a

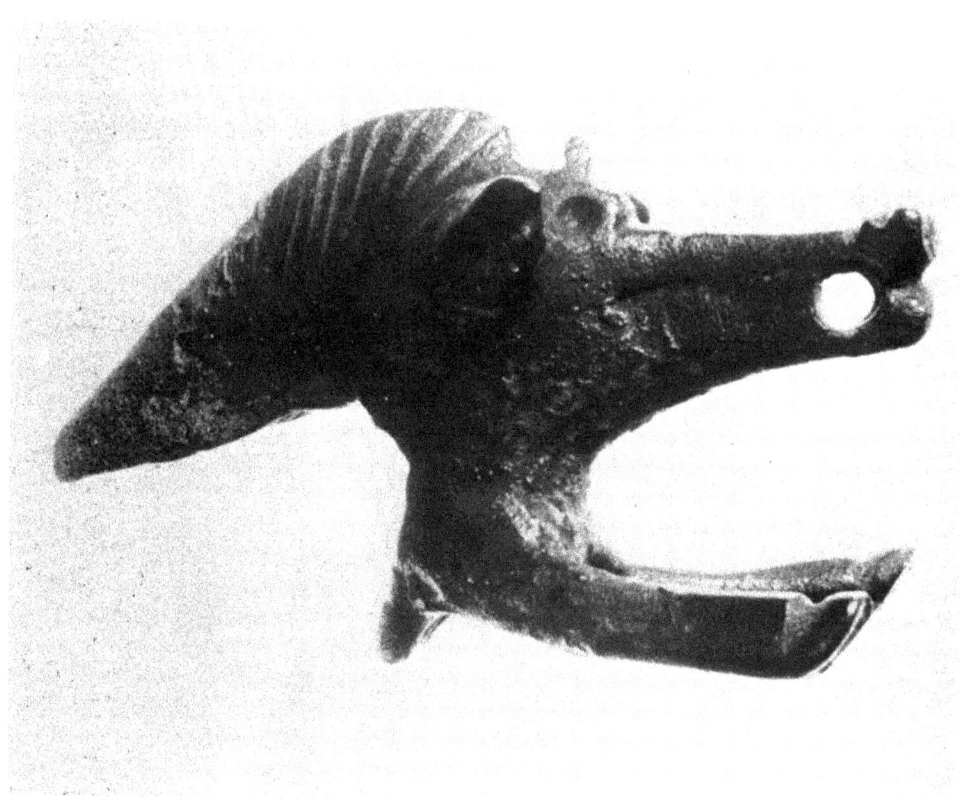

b

Plate X Boar forepart from London (Sydney Museum).

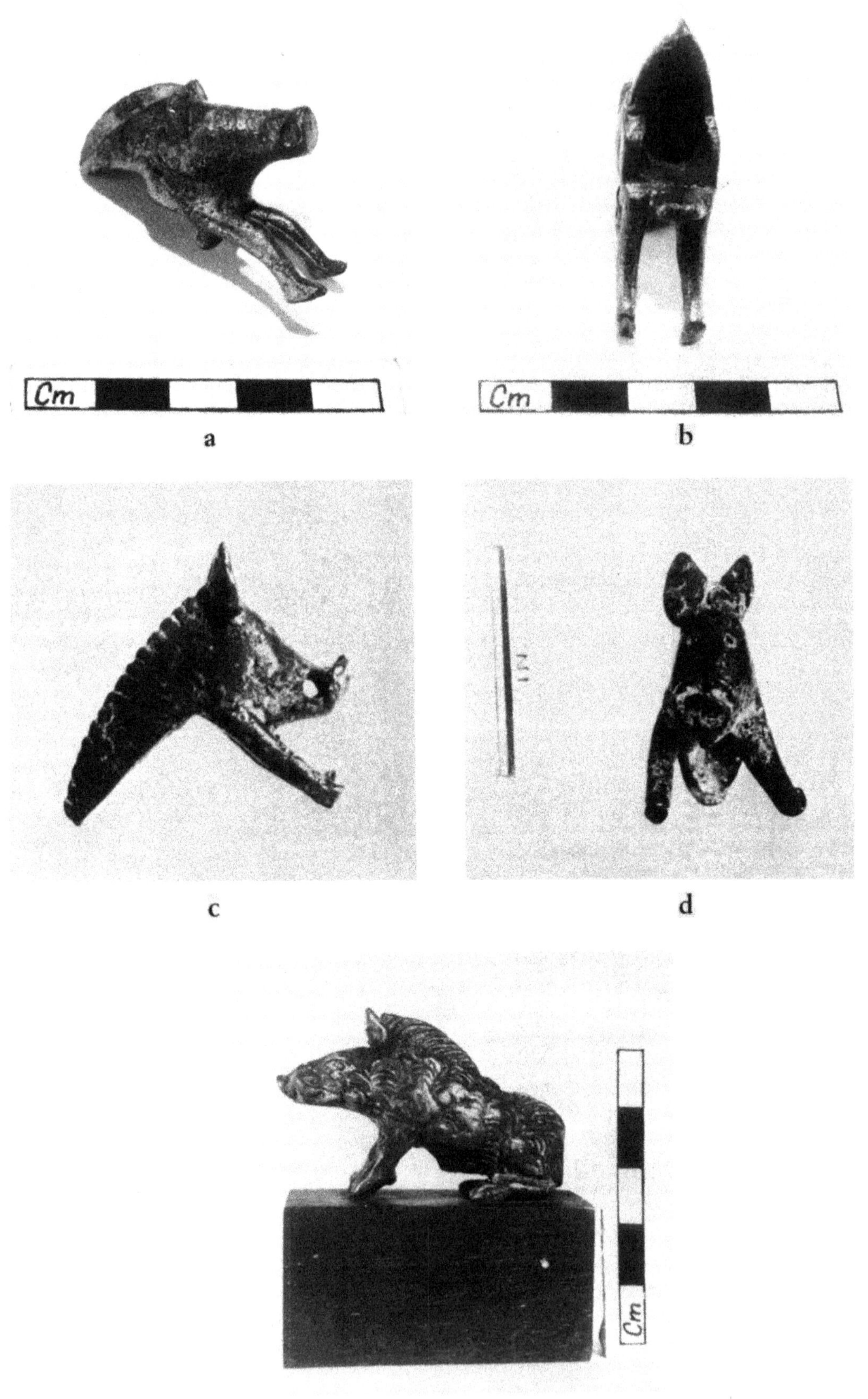

Plate XI Boar foreparts from Aldborough, Yorks. (a and b); Eastcheap, London (c and d); and figurine from Colchester, Essex (e).

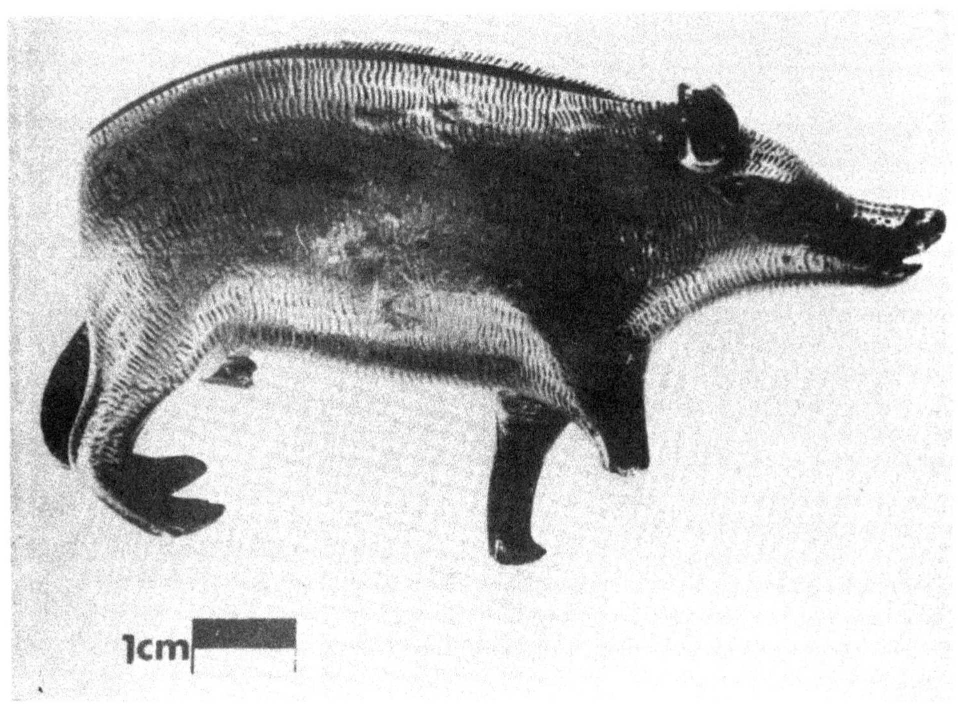

a

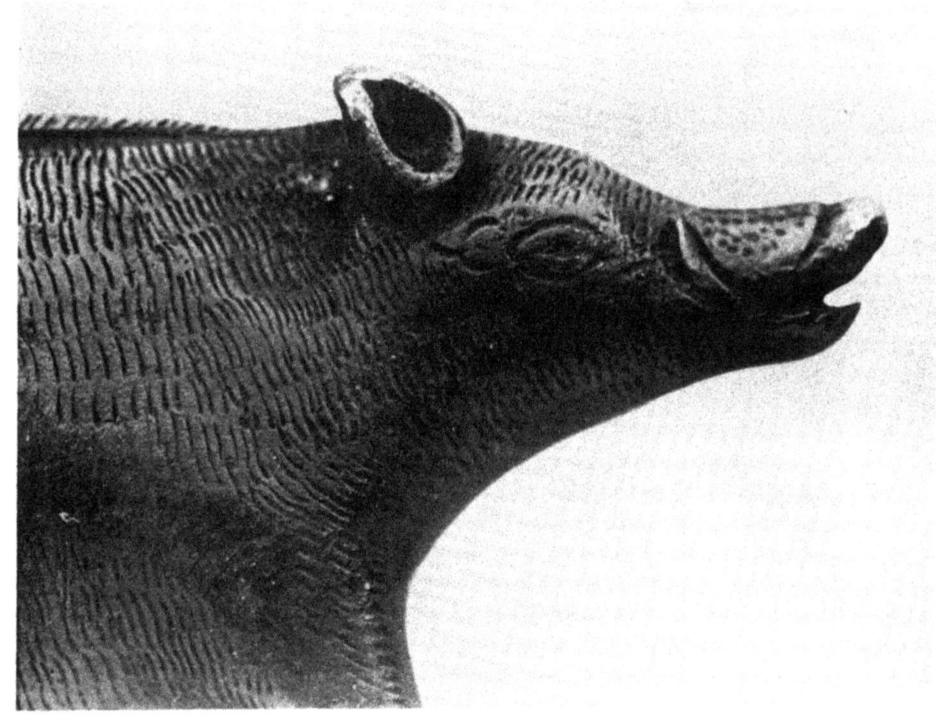

b

Plate XII Boar figurine from Ireland (W11).

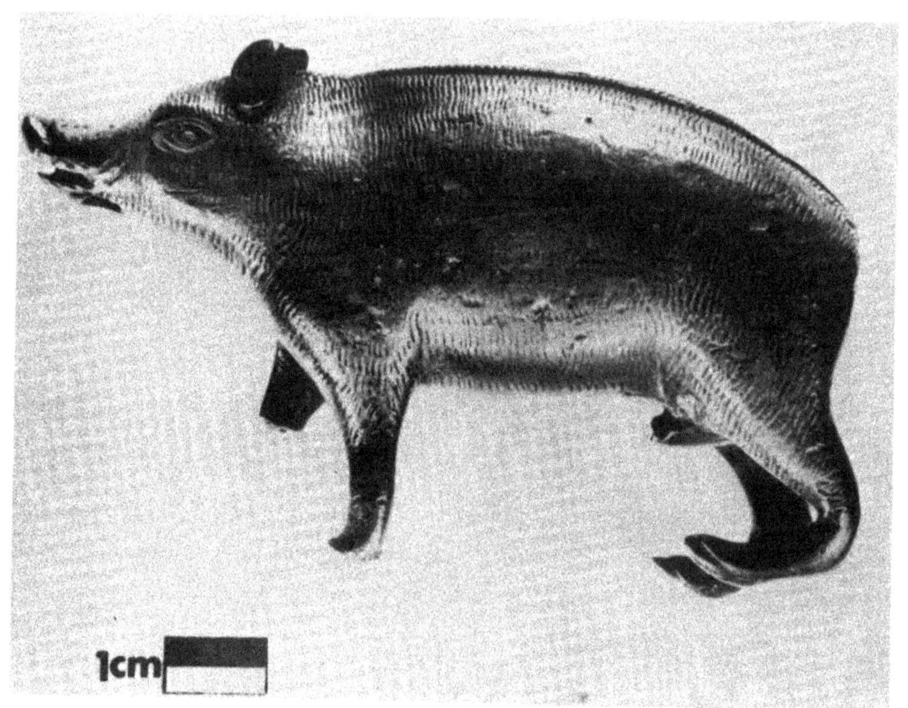

a

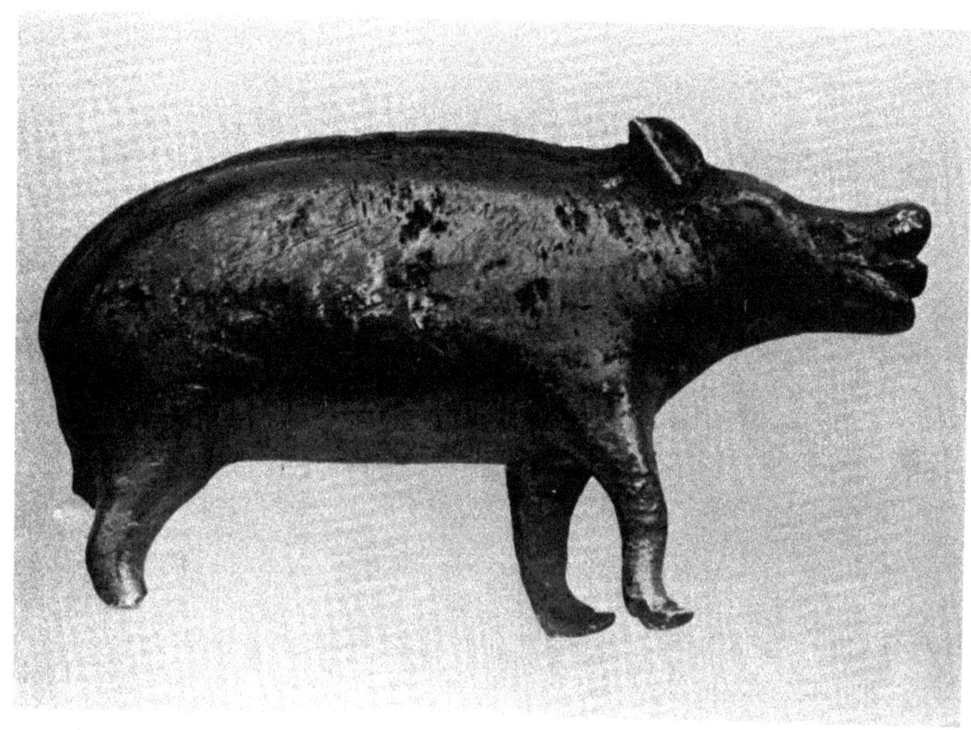

b

Plate XIII Boar figurines from Ireland (a: W11, b: W10).

CATALOGUE OF BRONZE BOAR FIGURINES FROM THE CONTINENT

1. Altenburg-Rheinau, Germany

Late Iron Age Oppidum, Context: pit.

Length, 7.4 cm; Height, 3.8 cm.

Ring in tail.

Ref. Fischer F., 1974 Einige Neufunde aus dem Spätkeltischen oppidum von Altenburg-Rheinau. Archäologisches Korrespondenzblatt 4, Heft 2, 159, Taf 33 (6).

2. Balzers, Gutenberg, Liechtenstein

Oppidum; cult place within the oppidum.

Height, 1 5/8".

Ref. Törbrügge, W., 1968, Prehistoric European Art (Abrams) 206; Megaw, 1970.129; Historical Collection, Vaduz.

3. Báta, Hungary

Length, 10.9 cm; Height, 7.8 cm.

Ref. Szabó, M., 1971. The Celtic Heritage in Hungary. (Budapest); Hunyady, I. von, 1942-44 Die Kelten in Karpatenbecken. Vol. 2 (Budapest), Taf., XXXVIII, 4.

Nemzeti National Museum of Hungary, Budapest.

4. Cahors, France

Bronze figure of a wild sow.

Espérandieu, E., 1925. Le recueil général des bas-reliefs, statues et bustes de la Gaule Romaine (Paris), IX; 264, No. 7049.

St. Germain-en-Laye Museum.

5. Gurina, Kärnten, Austria

Meyer, A. B., 1885 Gurina in Obergailthal (Kärnten) (Dresden) Taf. XI

6. Metz, Lorraine, France

Drack, W., 1954 Ein Mitteilateneschwert mit drei Goldmarken von Bottstein (Aargau) Zeitschrift f. Schweizerische Archäologie und Kunstgechichte 1954/55, 193-225, Taf. 61.

7. Joeuvres, Loire, France. Oppidum

Holes for suspension in crest.

Cabotze, J., 1966, Roanne à 2000 ans. Les Origines celtiques et gallo-romaines (Roanne), 125-6.

Déchelette, J., 1927 Manuel D'Archéologie, Vol. IV (Paris), 815, Fig. 568.

Musée J. Déchelette de Roanne.

8. Landonesq (Aveyron)

Drack, W., 1954 Ein Mittellatenèschwert mit drei Goldmarken von Böttstein (Aargau). Zeitschrift f. Schweizerische Archäologie und Kunstgeschichte. 1954/55, 193-225, Taf. 61.

9. Luncani (Grînd), Rumania

105 mm long.

Easternmost boar of Celtic workmanship, openwork crest.

Daicoviciu, C., 1960 Istoria Rominiei (Bucarest), 234, Fig. 55, 1.
Renard, M., 1966 Dieu au sanglier du Musée National d'Antiquités de Bucarest. Mélanges d'archéologie et d'histoire offerts à André Piganiol, R. Chevallier (ed.), Vol. 3, 1367-72 (Paris).

10. Luxembourg, The Titelberg oppidum

Surface find, 19th century.

Reinach, S., 1894 Bronzes figurés de la Gaule Romaine.

(Musée de Saint Germain-en-Laye), 267-8, No. 265

Thomas, H. L., 1975. The Titelberg: A Hill Fort of Celtic and Roman Times. Archaeology, Jan. 1975, 28, No. 1, 55-57.

Louvre Museum, Paris.

11. Mérida, Spain

Bronze cult chariot showing mounted man and dog pursuing wild boar on wheeled platform; length 25 cm.

Dillon and Chadwick, 1973, The Celtic Realms, Pl. 5.

Megaw, 1970, P1, 37.

St. Germain-en-Laye, Musée des Antiquités, France.

12. Mezek, Istanbul

Jacobsthal, 1944, Pl. 260g.

13. La Neuville-en-Hez (Forêt de Hez), Oise, France

Single find between 1812 - 1860.

Houbigant, A. G., 1860. Receuil des antiquités bellovaques conservées dans le cabinet de M. Houbigant, à Nogent-les-Vierges (Beauvais), 11-15, Pl. 1.

14. Neuvy-en-Sullias, France

Height, 68 cm, (Sheet metal; also two other life size boars, cast bronze).

Filip, J., 1962 Celtic Civilisation and its Heritage, (Prague, New Horizons), 160.

Musée Historique de L'Orleanais, Orleans.

15. Praha-Sárka, Czechoslovakia

Length, 11.6 cm.

Poulík J. and Forman, W., 1956, Pravekė Umení (Prague), Fig. 136.

Narodni Museum, Praha.

16. Salzburg - Rainberg, Austria

Filip, J., (ibid.), 1960, 64, Fig. 14.

17. St. Germain-en-Laye, France

9" long, pierced through belly, as though for a shaft.

Barnwell, 1871 164.

18. Tábor, Bohemia

Length, 80 mm.

Filip, J., (ibid.), 1960, 64, Fig. 14.

Early Celtic Art Catalogue (Hayward Gallery Exhibition), 1970, 18, No. 90.

Okresni Museum, Tabor.

19. Vesontio, Besançon, France

Castan, A., 1870, Le Champ-de-Mars de Vesontio (Besançon)

Rev. Archéologique N.S. XXI, 1-18 and 94-103, P1.V.

ACKNOWLEDGEMENTS

I should like to thank Professor F. R. Hodson and Dr. Mansel Spratling for their help in my research, and particularly Mr. Martin Bell for his constant encouragement.

I am grateful to the staff of the following museums for giving me permission to draw and photograph the figurines: Aldborough Museum, Yorkshire; Ashmolean Museum, Oxford; Brighton Museum; British Museum; Cambridge Museum of Archaeology and Ethnography; Colchester and Essex Museum; Chesters Museum; Ipswich County Museum; Barbican House Museum, Lewes; London Museum; National Museum of Wales, Cardiff; Somerset County Museum, Taunton; Worthing Museum.

And to the following museums for sending me photographs: Ashmolean Museum (Plate IVa); London Museum (Plate XIc and d); National Museum of Ireland, Dublin (Plates XII and XIII); Nicholson Museum, Sydney (Plate X).

This research was originally presented as a dissertation for a B.A. degree at the Institute of Archaeology, London.

ABBREVIATIONS

Acta Arch.	Acta Archaeologica
A.N.L.	Archaeological Newsletter
Ant.	Antiquity
Ant. J.	Antiquaries Journal
Arch.	Archaeologia
Arch. Ael.	Archaeologia Aeliana
Arch. Camb.	Archaeologia Cambrensis
Arch. J.	Archaeological Journal
Bristol & Glos. Arch. Soc.	Transactions of the Bristol and Gloucestershire Archaeological Society
B.U S.S.	Proceedings of the Bristol University Spelaeological Society
Inst. Arch. Occ. Paper	Institute of Archaeology, Occasional Paper
J.A.S.	Journal of Archaeological Science
J.B.A.A.	Journal of the British Archaeological Association
J.R.S.	Journal of Roman Studies
J.R.S.A.I.	Journal of the Royal Society of the Antiquaries of Ireland
Med. Arch.	Medieval Archaeology
P.P.S.	Proceedings of the Prehistoric Society
Proc. Cambs. Ant. Soc.	Proceedings of the Cambridgeshire Antiquarian Society
Proc. Hants. Field Club	Proceedings of the Hampshire Field Club
Proc. Roy. Irish Acad.	Proceedings of the Royal Irish Academy
Proc. Soc. Ant. L.	Proceedings of the Society of the Antiquaries of London
Proc. Som. Arch. & Nat. Hist. Soc.	Proceedings of the Somerset Archaeological and Natural History Society
Proc. Suff. Inst. Arch. & Nat. Hist.	Proceedings of the Suffolk Institute of Archaeology and Natural History

Sussex Arch. Coll.	Sussex Archaeological Collections
Sy. Arch. Coll.	Surrey Archaeological Collections
Trans. L. & Mx. Arch. Soc.	Transactions of the London and Middlesex Archaeological Society
Trans. Worcs.	Transactions of the Worcestershire Archaeological Society

BIBLIOGRAPHY

Allen, D. F., 1961, The origins of coinage in Britain: a reappraisal: in Problems of the Iron Age, ed. S. S. Frere (Occ. Paper 11, Inst. Arch.)

Armstrong, E. C. R., 1923, The La Tène period in Ireland, J.R.S.A.I. 53, 1-33.

Avery, M., et. al. 1967, Rainsborough, Northants, England. P.P.S., 33, 207-306.

Avery, M., 1968, Excavations at Meare East, Som. Arch. & Nat. Hist. Soc. (Proc. of) 112,21-39.

Barnwell, E. L., 1871, Bronze Boar, Arch. Camb. 4 ser. II, 163-7.

Beowulf, trans. K. C. Holland (MacMillan, 1968).

Boardman, J., Brown, M A., and Powell, T. G. E., (eds). 1971, The European Community in Later Prehistory (Routledge and Kegan Paul).

Bökönyi, S., 1974, History of Domestic Mammals in Central and Eastern Europe. (Budapest).

Bradley, R., 1968, Excavations on Portsdown Hill, 1963-5, Proc. Hants. Field Club, 24, 42-58.

Brailsford, J. W., 1953, Later Prehistoric Antiquities of the British Isles in the British Museum (H. M. S. O.)

Bruce-Mitford, R., 1974, Aspects of Anglo-Saxon Archaeology (London).

Burstow, G. P. & Holleyman, G. A., 1955, Excavations at Muntham Court, Findon, Sussex. A.N.L. March, 1955, 5, No. 10, 204-5; 1957, Excavations at Muntham Court, Findon, Sussex, A.N.L., 6, No. 4. 101-102; 1958, Plate in A.N.L., 6, No. 7, 170.

Clifford, E. M. 1961, Bagendon - a Belgic Oppidum (Cambridge).

Cunliffe, B. W., 1961, Report on a Belgic and Roman site at the Causeway, Horndean. Proc. Hants. Field Club 22, 25-29.

Cunliffe, B. W., 1968, Excavations at Eldon's Seat, Encombe, Dorset, P.P.S., 34, 191-237.

Cunliffe, B. W., 1973, The Regni, (Duckworth).

Cunliffe, B. W., 1974, Iron Age Communities in Britain, (Routledge and Kegan Paul).

Curwen, E.C., 1954, The Archaeology of Sussex (2nd ed. Methuen).

Déchelette, J., 1927, Manuel d'Archéologie Préhistorique, Vol. IV (Paris).

Doubleday, H A. & Page, W. (eds.) 1904, Victoria History of the Counties of England: Warwickshire. Vol. 1. (Haymarket, London).

Dunning, G. C., 1935, The swan's neck and ring-headed pins of the Early Iron Age in Britain. Arch. J. XCI, 269-295.

Fordham, H. G. 1904, A small bronze object found near Guilden Morden, Cambs. Proc. Cambs. Ant. Soc., X, 1901-4, 373 and 404.

Foster, J. A. A., 1977, A Boar Figurine from Guilden Morden, Cambs. Med. Arch. (forthcoming).

Foster, J. A. A., (in preparation), The Lexden Tumulus.

Fox, C., 1958, Pattern and Purpose: A Survey of Early Celtic Art in Britain, (Cardiff).

Franks, A. W., 1864, Account of additions to the British Museum in 1864. Proc. Soc. Ant. L., Series 2, Vol, III, 90-92.

Frend, W. H. C., 1955. Religion in Roman Britain in the fourth century A.D. J.B.A.A. (3rd Ser.), XVIII, 1-17 (Appendix, p.17).

Gray, H. St. George and Bulleid, A., 1953, The Meare Lake Village, Vol. 2, (published privately at Taunton Castle).

Greenwell, W., 1906, Early Iron Age Burials in Yorkshire. Arch. 60, 251-324.

Grimes, W. F., 1930 Holt, Denbighshire (Magazine of the Hon. Soc. of Cymmrodorion, London).

Hamilton, J. R. C., 1956, Excavations at Jarlshof, Shetland (H.M.S.O., Edinburgh).

Hamilton, J. R. C., 1968 Excavations at Clickhimin, Shetland (H.M.S.O., London).

Hastings, F., 1966, Excavation of an Iron Age farmstead at Hawk's Hill, Leatherhead, Sy. A. C., 62, 1-43.

Hawkes, C. F. C., 1959, The ABC of the British Iron Age, Ant., 33, 170-82.

Henry, F., 1940, Irish Art in the Early Christian Period (Methuen).

Higgs, E., and White, J., 1963, Autumn Killing, Ant. 37, 282-289.

Hodgson, G., 1961, Catcote, Northumberland, Arch. Ael. XLVI.

Hughes, M. J. M., 1972, A technical study of opaque red glass of the Iron Age in Britain, P.P.S. 38, 98-107.

Jacobsthal, P., 1944, Early Celtic Art (Oxford, Clarendon Press), 2 Vols.

Jesson, M., and Hill, D., (eds) 1971, The Iron Age and its Hillforts (Southampton).

Jope, E. M., 1961, Beginnings of La Tène ornamental style in the British Isles, in Problems of the Iron Age in Southern Britain, ed. S. S. Frere, 69-83 (Inst. Arch. Occ. Paper No. 11).

Kendrick, T. D., 1938, Anglo-Saxon Art to A.D.900. (Methuen).

Kenyon, K. M., 1953, Sutton Walls, Hereford. Arch. J. CX, 1f.

Klindt-Jensen, O., 1961. Gundestrup Kedelen (National Museum of Copenhagen Publications.).

Laver, P. G., 1927, The Excavation of a Tumulus at Lexden, Colchester. Arch. LXXVI, 241-254.

Leeds, E. T., 1933, Celtic Ornament (Oxford)

Lethbridge, T. C., 1953, Burial of an Iron Age warrior at Snailwell, Cambs. Proc. Cambs. Ant. Soc. 47, 25-37.

Liou, B., 1973, Recherches archeologiques sous-marines. Gallia, 31, 1973, 595-8.

Liversidge, J., 1968, Britain in the Roman Empire (London, Routledge and Kegan Paul).

Lower, M. A., and Chapman, R., 1866. Antiquities Preserved in the Society's Museum at Lewes Castle, Sussex Arch. Coll. XVIII, 60-73.

Mack, R. P., 1964, The Coinage of Ancient Britain, (London 2nd ed.)

Map of Southern Britain in the Iron Age. (Ordnance Survey, 1975).

Megaw, J. V. S., 1963, A British bronze bowl of the Belgic Iron Age from Poland, Ant. J. XLIII, 27-37.

Megaw, J. V. S., 1969, Two native bronzes of the Roman period from London, in the Nicholson Museum, Sydney, Trans. L. & Mx. Arch. Soc., 22, 45-47.

Megaw, J. V. S., 1970, Art of the European Iron Age: A study of the elusive image (Bath).

Moore, I., 1947, Roman Suffolk, Proc. Suff. Inst. Arch. and Nat. Hist. XXIV, 1946-8 (49), 163-179.

Oswald, A., 1972, Excavations at Beckford, Worcs. Trans. Worcs., 3, 7-53.

Parker, H. M. D., 1958. The Roman Legions (Cambridge).

Peacock, D. P. S., 1969, A contribution to the study of Glastonbury ware from South-western Britain. Ant. J. XLIX, 41-61.

Peacock, D. P. S., 1971, Roman amphorae in pre-Roman Britain, cf. The Iron Age and its Hillforts, Jesson & Hill (eds.), 161f.

Piggot, S., 1959, The Carnyx in Early Iron Age Britain. Ant. J. XXXIX, 19-32.

Piggott, S., 1965, Ancient Europe (Edinburgh University Press).

Pitt-Rivers, A., 1887 Excavations in Cranbourne Chase, Vol. 4, (Privately printed, London).

Pollexfen, J. H., 1863, Antiquities found at Colchester. Arch. 39(2), 508-510.

Powell, T. G. E., 1958, The Celts, (London, Thames and Hudson).

Powell, T. G. E., 1971, From Urartu to Gundestrup: the agency of Thracian Metal work. The European Community... (ed. Boardman et. al.), 183f.

Rahtz, P. & Brown, J., 1959, Blaise Castle H'll, Bristol, 1957. B.U.S.S. 8, 147-71.

R.C. H.M., 1911, An Inventory of the Ancient Monuments in Wales and Monmouthshire: 1 - County of Montgomery. (London H.M.S.O.)

Rees, A., and Rees, B., 1961, Celtic Heritage (London, Thames and Hudson).

Richmond, I. A., 1958, (ed.) Roman and native in North Britain (London, Nelson).

Richmond, I. A., 1968, Hod Hill, Vol. 2 (London).

Rivet, A. L. F., 1958, Town and Country in Roman Britain, (London, Hutchinson).

Ross, A., 1967, Pagan Celtic Britain (London, Routledge and Kegan Paul).

Ross, A., 1968, Shafts, pits and wells - sanctuaries of the Belgic Britons? in Studies in Ancient Europe (ed. Coles and Simpson), 255-285. (Leicester University Press).

Rostovtseff, M., and Taylor, M. V., 1923, Commodus-Hercules in Britain. J.R.S., 13,91-109.

Smith, H. Ecroyd, 1852. Reliquiae Insurianae: the Remains of the Roman Isurium (now Aldborough, near Boroughbridge, Yorkshire), (London).

Stanford, S., 1974, Croft Ambrey. (Privately printed).

Stead, I. M., 1965, The La Tène Cultures of Eastern Yorkshire, (Yorkshire Philosophical Society).

Stead, I. M. , 1968, An Iron Age Hillfort at Grimthorpe, Yorkshire, P.P.S. 34, 148-90.

Szabo, M., 1971, The Celtic Heritage in Hungary (Budapest).

Thomas, C., 1961, The Animal Art of the Scottish Iron Age and its Origins Arch. J. CXVIII, 14f.

Tierney, J. T., 1959, The Celtic Ethnography of Posidonius. Proc. Roy. Irish Acad. 60, 1959-60, 189-275.

Toms, H. S., 1907, Celtic boar from Woodingdean, Proc. Soc. Ant. L. Series 2, XXI, 489-90.

Toms, H. S., 1918, Quoted in: Ancient Britons at Kemp Town. Brighton Herald, 5th Jan. 1918, Page 4, Col. 3.

Toynbee, J. M. C.,, 1964, Art in Britain under the Romans (Oxford, Clarendon Press).

Vulliamy, C. E., 1930, The Archaeology of Middlesex and London. (Methuen).

Wacher, J. S., 1964, Excavations at Breedon-on-the-Hill, Leics. Ant. J. 44, 122-42.

Wainwright, G., 1967a, Coygan Camp, (Cambrian, Archaeological Association).

Wainwright, G., 1967b, The excavation of an Iron Age hillfort on Bathampton Down, Somerset, Bristol and Glos. Arch. Soc., 86, 42-59.

Wainwright, G., 1968, The excavation of a Durotrigian Farmstead near Tollard Royal in Cranbourne Chase. P.P.S., 34, 102-47.

Wallis Budge, E. A., 1903 (ed.) An Account of the Roman Antiquities preserved in the museum at Chesters. (London).

Werner, J., 1949, Eberzier von Monceau - le-neuf. Acta Arch. 20, 248-257.

Werner, E., and Craddock, P. T., 1971, Scientific Report on the Quantitative analysis of 10 late Iron Age and Romano-British bronzes from the Colchester and Essex Museum. B.M.R.L. File No. 3166, 11th Nov. 1971. (Unpublished manuscript in Colchester and Essex Museum).

Wheeler, R. E. M., 1943, Maiden Castle, Dorset. (Oxford).

www.ingramcontent.com/pod-product-compliance
Lightning Source LLC
LaVergne TN
LVHW070534110826
845147LV00017BA/988

* 9 7 8 0 9 0 4 5 3 1 7 4 9 *